Individually Yours®

CONTENTS

WELCOME TO PREFERRED

6   Advisory Board, Preferred Hotels® & Resorts Worldwide

7   Letter from Preferred's Managing Director

8   Preferred's Standard of Excellence™

9   Preferred's Above Expectations™ Program

10   Preferred's Partners Program

11   *The Preferred Way* Magazine

WORLDWIDE LOCATIONS

Preferred's hotels and resorts are divided into the following regions: Canada/USA, Latin America/Caribbean, Europe, Africa and Asia/Pacific. Within each of these sections, the hotels and resorts are listed alphabetically: first, by country; second, state/province; third, city; and last, hotel name. For quick reference, refer to the index beginning on page 190.

12   ■ Canada/USA

116   ■ Latin America/Caribbean

132   ■ Europe

162   ■ Africa

166   ■ Asia/Pacific

HE'S ON AN ALL EXPENSE PAID VACATION. THE TROUBLE IS, HE'S PAYING FOR IT WITH YOUR MONEY.

INTRODUCING THE TRAVELFUNDS® CARD FROM AMERICAN EXPRESS,®
A NEW SAFE WAY TO CARRY MONEY. If your debit card ends up in someone else's hands, your vacation can, too. All the more reason to carry a TravelFunds Card. It's a prepaid, reloadable card that isn't linked to your bank account. If it's lost or stolen, your balance is refunded, usually within 24 hours. It can even help you replace lost passports and major credit cards.* Best of all, it's accepted at millions of places worldwide, including ATMs. Make sure your next vacation is really yours.
Call 1-866-AMEX-TFC or visit www.americanexpress.com/travelfundscard

DON'T LEAVE HOME WITHOUT IT.®

CONTENTS

MEETING PLANNING, SPAS & RESORT HOTEL AMENITIES

170   Meeting Planning
178   Resort Amenities & Spas
187   Source for Travel and Meeting Professionals:
Preferred Sales Offices
188   General Information
204   Worldwide Reservations Information

INDEXES

For quick reference to a hotel or resort by city, region or name, please refer to one of the indexes below:

190   Hotels & Resorts by City
195   Hotels & Resorts by Region
     195 Africa
     195 Asia/Pacific
     195 Canada/USA
     197 Europe
     198 Latin America/Caribbean
199   Hotels & Resorts by Name

CONTACT US

To learn more about Preferred's partnerships and programs, complete and return the reply card located on the inside back cover or forward your inquiry to:

Preferred Hotels® & Resorts Worldwide
311 South Wacker Drive, Suite 1900
Chicago, Illinois 60606 USA
Tel: +1 312 913 0400 Fax: +1 312 913 0444
info@preferredhotels.com
www.preferredhotels.com

CHECK IN
to the world of haute hotels

The more you want out of your holiday, the more you need a Virtuoso travel specialist. We know the world and all the ways for you to discover it.

As our client, hundreds of the world's finest hotels, resorts, spas and lodges will roll out the red carpet for you. We'll get you into the right hotel, in the right room, with the right view . . . when others can't. You'll also enjoy upgrades and special amenities or services at no additional cost — all as our guest.

PREFERRED ADVISORY BOARD

Photographed from left to right

MR. STEPHAN J.A.B. STOKKERMANS
Commercial Director
Grand Hotel Huis ter Duin
Amsterdam/Noordwijk aan Zee
The Netherlands

MR. SAYED M. SALEH
President & Managing Director
The Orchards Hotel
Williamstown, Massachusetts USA

MR. ROBERT M. CORNELL
Managing Director
Preferred Hotels® & Resorts Worldwide
Chicago, Illinois USA

MR. MARK J. NOVOTA
Managing Partner
Wequassett Inn Resort & Golf Club
Cape Cod, Massachusetts USA

MR. ANTON J. PIRINGER
Vice President, Hospitality
Vail Resorts, Inc.
Vail, Colorado USA

MR. WILLIAM J. OTTO
President
Marcus Hotels and Resorts
Milwaukee, Wisconsin USA
Chairman, Preferred Advisory Board

A LETTER FROM THE MANAGING DIRECTOR

Dear Guest:

I am frequently asked, what makes a hotel a Preferred hotel and how are Preferred hotels different? Having stayed at nearly all of our hotels personally, I can testify that there is a core commitment within our ranks to maintain a positive attitude toward service. We refer to this as the "Preferred Experience." Each of our 1,600 standards and practices is adopted by our hotels in a special way that takes maximum advantage of their unique locations and facilities. Be it a bustling city center or a remote resort destination, you can be assured that you will receive the same unsurpassed service and response to all of your needs during your stay.

The 123 Preferred hotels presented in this directory have been selected through an extensive process of evaluations, on-site inspections and random service checks to assure that they meet Preferred's Standards of Excellence™ quality assurance program. They have all earned the privilege of displaying the coveted Preferred plaque on their door, which is a sign of their commitment to the highest standards. As each hotel is re-inspected every year, these standards must be maintained at all times.

As we endeavor to improve the overall level of quality and options for guests of Preferred, we continue to add new hotels that meet the rigorous Preferred standards. By the same token, if a hotel is unable or unwilling to operate at the high standards we require, they are asked to leave Preferred. To make sure that our hotels meet these requirements, Preferred's field inspectors assume the identity of regular hotel guests in order to anonymously check each item and verify their application to the needs of today's discerning travelers. In fact, frequent users of Preferred are often the best judges of whether or not a hotel belongs among our ranks, and we welcome your comments and suggestions at any time.

How many Preferred hotels have you experienced, and which are your favorites? Please let us know by visiting our Web site, www.preferredhotels.com, and filling out your own evaluation. Your comments will be considered when it is time to select Preferred's Hotel of the Year.

We look forward to welcoming you, and welcoming you back very soon.

Sincerely,

Robert M. Cornell

Robert M. Cornell
Managing Director

Preferred Hotels® & Resorts Worldwide
Tel: +1 312 913 0400 Fax: +1 312 913 0444
E-mail: info@preferredhotels.com

PREFERRED'S STANDARDS OF EXCELLENCE™ PROGRAM

To become a Preferred member, hotels must adhere to Preferred's award-winning Standards of Excellence™ program, an exhaustive quality-assurance program that includes an annual, third-party-unannounced audit of 1,600 standards and practices. As a result of this unique program, guests consistently receive the highest levels of attentive service and luxurious accommodations at all Preferred hotels and resorts.

To ensure that the Preferred standards are current, several of our experienced hotel managers serve on the Quality Assurance Committee. The Quality Assurance Committee meets on a regular basis to discuss travel trends and developments that may affect our regular travelers.

Each year, refinements are made to our inspection checklist to reflect the needs of our guests, and hotels are notified to change their training programs to reflect any modifications.

If you have any ideas or suggestions on how our program can be further enhanced, please visit our Web site at www.preferredhotels.com and let us know your thoughts.

PREFERRED HOTELS & RESORTS SERVICES
"ABOVE EXPECTATIONS"

As part of Preferred's Standards of Excellence™ quality-assurance program, our licensed quality assurance inspectors take special care to examine three categories of Preferred hotel amenities that you, our guests, have found very important:

FAMILY SERVICE AMENITIES

For travelers with infants and younger children, hotels displaying this icon welcome children and are prepared to offer such items as cribs, children's menus, games and child care services.

HEALTH AND FITNESS FACILITIES

For travelers who wish to maintain a fitness regimen while on the road, hotels displaying this icon provide supervised facilities with access to cardio-vascular equipment, resistance training equipment and free weights.

@ TELECOMMUNICATIONS

For travelers who wish to stay connected while on the road, hotels displaying this icon are equipped with telecommunications capabilities that allow travelers to conduct simultaneous voice and digital communications from their guestroom or a business center in the hotel.

PET SERVICES

For travelers with properly trained household pets, hotels displaying this icon are pet-friendly and provide services and amenities to accommodate guests with pets.

THE CONFERENCE COLLECTION

Many Preferred hotels and resorts are specially equipped to handle meetings and conferences ranging in size from a board meeting of 10 to banquets for 1,000 persons. These hotels meet certain minimum standards specific to meeting and conference services, and therefore are designated with the Conference Collection icon. This special designation means that you can be confident that participating hotels have the experience and capabilities to provide professional services and amenities to meeting planners and attendees.

LEGEND

Conference Collection

Family Services

Health and Fitness

Pet Services

@ Internet and Telecommunications

9

PREFERRED PARTNERS

Preferred is committed to partnering with highly recognized brands to enhance the travel experience and bring more value to our guests. Our objective is to partner with prestigious brands that can enhance an already memorable experience — one that is as unique and distinct as each of our independently owned hotels and resorts.

Preferred maintains relationships with the following Marketing Partners:

UNITED
Mileage Plus.

Through Preferred's partnership with United Airlines Mileage Plus®, Mileage Plus members can earn 500 bonus miles per stay at all Preferred hotels and resorts. To qualify, please identify yourself as a United Mileage Plus member and provide your membership number at check-in.*

Alaska Airlines

Many Preferred hotels and resorts on the West Coast of North America are partners in Alaska Airlines' Mileage Plan program. Mileage Plan members can earn 500 miles per stay at any participating hotel or resort. To qualify, please identify yourself as an Alaska Airlines

Mileage Plan member and provide your membership number at check-in. For a list of participating properties, please visit the Preferred Web site at www.preferredhotels.com.*

 Cards

The American Express® Card is warmly welcomed at all Preferred hotels and resorts. No matter which Preferred hotel or resort you visit around the world, the American Express Card is one of the most recognized forms of payment.

 THE WALL STREET JOURNAL.

Preferred partners with *USA Today* and the *Wall Street Journal* to bring quality amenities and services to all of our business and leisure guests.

For up-to-date details on Preferred's new Marketing Partners, visit us at: www.preferredhotels.com

*If you are a member of more than one of the mentioned programs, points may be claimed in only one program per paid stay.

CELEBRATE LUXURY LIFESTYLE WITH
THE PREFERRED WAY MAGAZINE

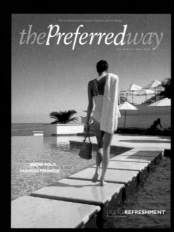

The Preferred Way magazine is a celebration of today's luxury lifestyle. This upscale publication brings you, the Preferred guest, lively and informative articles on the world's best food and wine, fashion, travel destinations and, of course, the most distinctive luxury hotels and resorts in the world. Published by Preferred Hotels® & Resorts Worldwide, *The Preferred Way* is available in the guestrooms of every Preferred property worldwide. Please accept and enjoy your copy of *The Preferred Way* with our compliments.

The United States
& Canada

METROPOLITAN HOTEL, VANCOUVER

An intimate refuge at the vibrant center of Vancouver's financial, shopping and entertainment districts. Guests are surrounded with classic contemporary styling and elegant décor in a cosmopolitan setting. Downtown, just steps from Pacific Centre, Queen Elizabeth Theatre and Robson Street shops. Vancouver Int'l. Airport: 9 miles/ 14 km, 25 minutes.

ACCOMMODATIONS: 197 total guestrooms, including 16 suites, each with oversized marble bathrooms, soaker tubs, separate walk-in showers, Frette bathrobes, high-speed broadband connectivity access, two dual-line phones, voice mail, newspaper, fully stocked bars and opening windows.

FACILITIES/SERVICES: Les Clefs d'Or Concierge, squash, indoor pool, whirlpool, saunas, massage therapy, downtown limousine service, fitness center and dry cleaning.

BUSINESS SERVICES: Business Center with translating services, high-speed broadband connectivity, video teleconferencing and audio-visual services.

DINING: "Diva at the Met" award-winning restaurant, lounge and patio, a celebrated local favorite offering Pacific Northwest originality.

MEETINGS: Total Meeting Rooms: 7 Total Sq. Ft.: 7,800 / Sq. M.: 726

RATES: CAD 335.00 to 3,000.00; Corporate, Group, Package rates.

Mr. Tom Waithe, General Manager

645 Howe Street
Vancouver, British Columbia V6C 2Y9, Canada
Tel: +1 604 687 1122
Fax: +1 604 689 7044
Email: reservations@metropolitan.com
www.metropolitan.com

Worldwide Reservations

www.preferredhotels.com

+800 323 7500 USA/Canada

+00 800 3237 5001 Europe (UIFN)

Other areas: See page 204

HOTEL GRAND PACIFIC

ACCOMMODATIONS: 304 total guestrooms, including 46 suites, each with balcony, duvets, bathrobes, newspaper, mini-bar, safe, hair dryer, coffee maker and video check-out. Ladies Executive Rooms available with additional amenities.

FACILITIES/SERVICES: Spa, health club, pool, Marine Adventure Center, concierge, in-room entertainment systems and complimentary parking.

BUSINESS SERVICES: Complimentary in-room Internet access, fax, photocopying, Business Center and secretarial services; Wi-Fi access available in public areas.

DINING: "The Pacific Restaurant" offers dishes with a Pacific Northwest flavor. "The Mark" is the signature restaurant featuring West Coast cuisine and fine wines. "The Courtyard Café" offers coffees and light fare.

MEETINGS: Total Meeting Rooms: 12 Total Sq. Ft.: 12,000 / Sq. M.: 1,117

RATES: CAD 229.00 to 1,200.00; Corporate, Group, Package rates.

Mr. Reid James, General Manager

463 Belleville Street
Victoria, British Columbia V8V 1X3,
Canada
Tel: +1 250 386 0450
Fax: +1 250 380 4474
Email: reserve@hotelgrandpacific.com
www.hotelgrandpacific.com

Located on Victoria's spectacular Inner Harbour, the Hotel Grand Pacific offers classical styling combined with European elegance. From the landscaped forecourt to the cascading water features and lobby with sparkling chandeliers, the hotel creates a harmonious and luxurious environment for each guest. Offering stunning views, original and commissioned artwork, exquisite service, and an ideal location next to the Legislative Buildings, the hotel is just steps from shopping, attractions, conference centre and business district.

Worldwide Reservations
www.preferredhotels.com
+800 323 7500 USA/Canada
+00 800 3237 5001 Europe (UIFN)
Other areas: See page 204

ARC THE.HOTEL

Comfort and luxury are paired with contemporary design in the serene and sophisticated ARC The.Hotel. The only design hotel in Canada's capital offers luxuriously appointed rooms in an intimate atmosphere, to ensure you feel energized and relaxed. Located in the heart of downtown Ottawa, ARC The.Hotel is central to government and corporate activity and is within walking distance of Parliament Hill, the Rideau Canal, Byward Market, and the National Gallery of Canada. MacDonald-Cartier Int'l. Airport: 7 miles/ 12 km, 20 minutes.

ACCOMMODATIONS: 112 total guestrooms, including 8 suites, each designed for tranquility and relaxation with Egyptian linens and Aveda amenities. Some with Roman tubs. All rooms feature data port, high-speed Internet access, two multi-line phones, voice mail, newspaper, CD player, safe, mini-bar, robes and hair dryer. VCR available on request.

FACILITIES/SERVICES: Sparkling wine on arrival, turndown service with Godiva chocolates, spring water and signature green apples. Starbucks coffee and Tazo tea, CD library and magazine selection, 24-hour health club, spa, concierge, child care, dry cleaning and daily parking.

BUSINESS SERVICES: Business Center and translating services.

DINING: "ARC Lounge" creates a world of chic regional Canadian cuisine in a hip atmosphere.

MEETINGS: Total Meeting Rooms: 3 Total Sq. Ft.: 1,195 / Sq. M.: 111

RATES: CAD 179.00 to 425.00 ; Corporate, Group, Package rates.

Mr. Guy Luzy, General Manager

140 Slater Street
Ottawa, Ontario K1P 5H6, Canada
Tel: +1 613 238 2888
Fax: +1 613 238 0053
Email: reservations@arcthehotel.com
www.arcthehotel.com

Worldwide Reservations
www.preferredhotels.com
+800 323 7500 USA/Canada
+00 800 3237 5001 Europe (UIFN)
Other areas: See page 204

METROPOLITAN HOTEL, TORONTO

ACCOMMODATIONS: 422 total guestrooms, including 58 suites, each with European linens and down duvets, broadband connectivity, two dual-line phones, computer/fax, data port, voice mail, fully stocked bar and opening windows.

FACILITIES/SERVICES: Les Clefs d'Or Concierge, fitness center, pool, whirlpool, massage, dry cleaning, turndown service and downtown limousine service.

BUSINESS SERVICES: On-site Business Center with state-of-the-art equipment, broadband connectivity, videoconferencing and audiovisual services.

DINING: "Hemispheres Restaurant and Bistro" has redefined haute cuisine with the freshest, most exciting influences from around the world. Reflecting the exotic ingredients of the Pacific Rim, "Lai Wah Heen" serves the finest Cantonese cuisine in an elegant atmosphere.

MEETINGS: Total Meeting Rooms: 17 Total Sq. Ft.: 13,000 / Sq. M.: 1,210

RATES: CAD 300.00 to 2,100.00; Corporate, Group, Package rates.

Mr. Jeremy Roncoroni,
General Manager

108 Chestnut Street
Toronto, Ontario M5G 1R3, Canada
Tel: +1 416 977 5000
Fax: +1 416 977 9513
Email: reservations@metropolitan.com
www.metropolitan.com

A contemporary hotel in the heart of downtown Toronto, where guests will enjoy exceptional service, outstanding amenities, exquisite dining and remarkable pleasures. Downtown, adjacent to City Hall, within walking distance of the city's financial, commercial and cultural heart. Minutes from the Toronto Eaton Centre, the Royal Ontario Museum, the Art Gallery of Ontario, SkyDome, premier theater and Toronto attractions. Pearson Int'l. Airport: 15 miles/25 km, 30 minutes.

Worldwide Reservations
www.preferredhotels.com
+800 323 7500 USA/Canada
+00 800 3237 5001 Europe (UIFN)
Other areas: See page 204

SOHO METROPOLITAN HOTEL

Welcome to the newest luxury hotel in Toronto. The moment you set foot upon the marble floors of the SoHo Met, you enter a world of exquisite delights and unparalleled convenience, where commitment to service and personal attention exceeds all expectations. The SoHo Met is quite simply Toronto's finest. In the heart of Toronto's entertainment, theater and financial districts. Pearson Int'l. Airport: 10 miles/16 km, 25 minutes.

ACCOMMODATIONS: 88 total guestrooms, including 17 suites, and a three-story loft-style penthouse overlooking the city. All rooms feature soaker tubs, separate showers, heated marble bathroom floors, Frette linens, in-room office, mini-bars, smart technology, broadband connectivity, wireless Internet access and DVD players.

FACILITIES/SERVICES: Les Clefs d'Or Concierge, 10,000-square-foot spa and state-of-the-art fitness center with steam room and lap pool.

BUSINESS SERVICES: On-site Business Center, state-of-the-art audiovisual equipment, broadband connectivity, wireless Internet access and limo service.

DINING: "Senses Restaurant" features captivating food and exceptional wine.

MEETINGS: Total Meeting Rooms: 2 Total Sq. Ft.: 2,230 / Sq. M.: 208

RATES: CAD 395.00 to 3,600.00; Corporate, Group, Package rates.

Ms. Nancy Munzar Kelly, Acting General Manager

318 Wellington Street West
Toronto, Ontario M5V 3T4, Canada
Tel: +1 416 599 8800
Fax: +1 416 599 8801
Email: soho@metropolitan.com
www.soho.metropolitan.com

Worldwide Reservations
www.preferredhotels.com
+800 323 7500 USA/Canada
+00 800 3237 5001 Europe (UIFN)
Other areas: See page 204

THE WYNFREY HOTEL AT RIVERCHASE GALLERIA

ACCOMMODATIONS: 329 total guestrooms, including 12 suites, each with automated mini-bar, wireless Internet access, data port, voice mail, Web TV, in-room games and movies, hair dryer, coffee maker and VCR available on request.

FACILITIES/SERVICES: Fitness center, concierge, spa, seasonal outdoor pool and Jacuzzi, complimentary airport transportation, salon, dry cleaning and shoe shine. Hotel attached to Riverchase Galleria.

BUSINESS SERVICES: On-site 24-hour Business Center, secretarial services available upon request, and Kinko's only steps away.

DINING: Choose Shula's Steak House for the "undefeated" experience you expect from the NFL's winningest coach, "Chicory Grille" for informal dining or "Ivory's" for cocktails.

MEETINGS: Total Meeting Rooms: 22 Total Sq. Ft.: 32,000 / Sq. M.: 2,793

RATES: USD 155.00 to 1,000.00; Corporate, Group, Package rates.

Mr. Danny Hiatt, General Manager

1000 Riverchase Galleria
Birmingham, Alabama 35244, USA
Tel: +1 205 987 1600
Fax: +1 205 987 9552
Email: sales@wynfreyhotel.com
www.wynfrey.com

From the sparkling French chandelier to the glistening Italian marble floors, this contemporary hotel was designed for luxury. Meticulously decorated with paintings and furnishings from the 1800s, the hotel is a Southern symbol of worldly elegance. The Wynfrey Hotel offers Southern hospitality and service with old-world charm. Attached to the spectacular Riverchase Galleria, which boasts 200 stores, 20 restaurants and 10 theaters. Birmingham Int'l. Airport: 20 miles/32 km, 25 minutes.

Worldwide Reservations
www.preferredhotels.com
+800 323 7500 *USA/Canada*
+00 800 3237 5001 *Europe (UIFN)*
Other areas: See page 204

HOTEL CAPTAIN COOK

Warm teak and polished brass details echo the nautical heritage of the hotel's namesake. This landmark is set against the spectacular backdrop of the Alaskan wilderness. In the heart of the downtown business and shopping districts. Ted Stevens Anchorage Int'l. Airport: 6 miles/10 km, 15 minutes.

ACCOMMODATIONS: 547 total guestrooms, including 96 suites, each with multi-line phones, data port, voice mail, robes, hair dryer, down comforter duvet, 250-thread-count linens, oversized down pillows and Neutrogena bath products.

FACILITIES/SERVICES: Indoor pool, Jacuzzi, racquetball, massage, full-service separate athletic club, dry cleaning, salon, shops, concierge, turndown service and Austrian consulate.

BUSINESS SERVICES: On-site Business Center available.

DINING: The award-winning "Crows Nest" for fine dining; "Fletcher's" and the "Pantry" for casual fare; "Whale's Tail Coffee & Spirits" for gourmet coffee, cocktails and light fare.

MEETINGS: Total Meeting Rooms: 14 Total Sq. Ft.: 18,507 / Sq. M.: 1,723

RATES: USD 135.00 to 1,500.00; Corporate, Group, Package rates.

Mr. Walter J. Hickel, President

4th Avenue at K Street
Anchorage, Alaska 99501, USA
Tel: +1 907 276 6000
Fax: +1 907 343 2298
Email: info@captaincook.com
www.captaincook.com

Worldwide Reservations

www.preferredhotels.com
+800 323 7500   USA/Canada
+00 800 3237 5001   Europe (UIFN)
Other areas: See page 204

ACCOMMODATIONS: 418 total guestrooms, including 22 suites, each with two multi-line phones, Internet access, data port, high-speed Internet access (May 2004), voice mail, hair dryer, and iron & board.

FACILITIES/SERVICES: Concierge services, fitness center, dry cleaning and gift shop.

BUSINESS SERVICES: On-site Business Center.

DINING: "Capriccio Grill" offers classic grilled steaks, seafood and traditional Italian favorites. "The Lobby Bar's" 42-foot granite bar is the social rendezvous. "Mallards" is an intimate bar with a club-like atmosphere.

MEETINGS: Total Meeting Rooms: 14 Total Sq. Ft.: 40,000 / Sq. M.: 3,724

RATES: USD 189.00 to 1,500.00; Corporate, Group, Package rates.

Mr. Timothy S. Gonser,
Vice President & General Manager

3 Statehouse Plaza
Little Rock, Arkansas 72201, USA
Tel: +1 501 906 4000
Fax: +1 501 375 4721
Email: sregan@peabodylittlerock.com
www.peabodylittlerock.com

The Peabody Little Rock opened in February 2002, following a $40-million renovation. Guests are welcomed into a truly inviting space, which is both dramatic and exquisitely comfortable. The lobby houses the famous Peabody Duck Fountain. Guestrooms are spacious and warm, and designed to please the most discerning of guests. Located in the heart of downtown Little Rock on the banks of the Arkansas River, the hotel is in the thriving River Market district, surrounded by historical and cultural attractions. Little Rock National Airport: 10 miles/16 km, 15 minutes.

Worldwide Reservations
www.preferredhotels.com
+800 323 7500 USA/Canada
+00 800 3237 5001 Europe (UIFN)
Other areas: See page 204

THE MOSAIC HOTEL BEVERLY HILLS

Nestled in the heart of Beverly Hills, only steps from Rodeo Drive and Century City, the recently remodeled Mosaic Hotel Beverly Hills is an oasis of elegance, warmth and impeccable service in a tranquil and intimate environment.

ACCOMMODATIONS: 47 total guestrooms, including 5 suites, each with two phones, voice mail, free DSL, newspaper, CD player, mini-bar, safe, hair dryer and robes.

FACILITIES/SERVICES: Fitness center with treadmill, StairMaster and free weights. Outdoor heated pool, spa, dry cleaning and concierge.

BUSINESS SERVICES: Secretarial and translating services available.

DINING: A full-service restaurant with an international flair featuring such specialties as Spanish tapas, Tuscan pan-fried polenta with pesto, and cuisine of the Far East.

RATES: USD 225.00 to 600.00; Corporate, Group, Package rates.

Mr. Brendan Carlin, General Manager

125 South Spalding Drive
Beverly Hills, California 90212, USA
Tel: +1 310 278 0303
Fax: +1 310 278 1728
Email: info@mosaichotel.com
www.mosaichotel.com

Worldwide Reservations
www.preferredhotels.com
+800 323 7500 USA/Canada
+00 800 3237 5001 Europe (UIFN)
Other areas: See page 204

ACCOMMODATIONS: 97 total guestrooms, including 14 suites, each with multi-line phones, data port, voice mail, Internet access, Wi-Fi, newspaper, complimentary refreshment bar, robes, hair dryer, DVD/CD player.

FACILITIES/SERVICES: Championship golf, hiking and jogging trails, spa, wellness center, fitness room, tennis, child care services, dry cleaning, shoe shine and shops.

DINING: "The Covey" offers contemporary cuisine overlooking the hills of Carmel. Enjoy views of lush fairways in the casual "Club Dining Room." Light snacks and beverages are served on "The Covey Deck" overlooking Mallard Lake. At "Edgar's Luxury Sports Bar" guests can sip a cocktail or sample the menu by renowned Cal Stamenov. Seasonal dishes with local ingredients will delight diners. Sports fans can check scores simultaneously on 12 flat-screen TVs situated throughout the restaurant.

MEETINGS: Total Meeting Rooms: 6 Total Sq. Ft.: 6,540 / Sq. M.: 609

RATES: USD 295.00 to 795.00; Corporate, Group, Package rates.

Mr. Bruce Pofahl, Resort Manager

8205 Valley Greens Drive
Carmel, California 93923, USA
Tel: +1 831 624 2888
Fax: +1 831 624 3726
Email: info@quaillodge.com
www.quaillodge.com

Quail Lodge Resort & Golf Club conveys a casual elegance with relaxed California style. Nestled among 850 acres of emerald green fairways, sparkling lakes and rolling hills, this resort offers a variety of recreational activities. On the sunny side of Carmel, this haven of serenity in harmony with nature awakens all the senses. Just five minutes from Carmel, on the Monterey Peninsula. Close to beaches and shopping. Monterey Peninsula Airport: 13 miles/21 km, 20 minutes.

Worldwide Reservations
www.preferredhotels.com
+800 323 7500 USA/Canada
+00 800 3237 5001 Europe (UIFN)
Other areas: See page 204

MONTAGE RESORT & SPA

Perched on the dramatic cliffs of Laguna Beach, Montage Resort & Spa is a beachside estate adorned in early twentieth-century style where every luxurious room offers sweeping ocean views. At Montage, unique memories are created and all requests are provided for with personalized service. Located in Laguna Beach, a world-renowned artist colony along the majestic coastline of the Pacific Ocean. John Wayne/Orange County Airport:18 miles/30 km, 20 minutes.

ACCOMMODATIONS: 262 total guestrooms, including 51 suites, each with three phones, data port, voice mail, bathrobes, complimentary newspaper, mini-bar, safe and hair dryer. All rooms have DVD/CD players and flat-screen televisions.

FACILITIES/SERVICES: Oceanfront spa, sauna, whirlpool, fitness center, salon, concierge services, shoe shine, child care services, dry cleaning and shops.

BUSINESS SERVICES: On-site Business Center with secretarial and translating services.

DINING: California-inspired Mediterranean cuisine served in the oceanfront signature restaurant "Studio," the casual "Loft," and poolside at "Mosaic Bar & Grille."

MEETINGS: Total Meeting Rooms: 8 Total Sq. Ft.: 14,500 / Sq. M.: 1,350

RATES: USD 475.00 to 5,500.00; Corporate, Group, Package rates.

Mr. James Bermingham, General Manager

30801 South Coast Highway
Laguna Beach, California 92651, USA
Tel: +1 949 715 6000
Fax: +1 949 715 6130
Email: reservations@
montagelagunabeach.com
www.montagelagunabeach.com

Worldwide Reservations
www.preferredhotels.com
+800 323 7500 USA/Canada
+00 800 3237 5001 Europe (UIFN)
Other areas: See page 204

SURF & SAND RESORT

ACCOMMODATIONS: 165 total guestrooms, including 13 suites, each with two phones, data port, voice mail, newspaper, CD player, safe, mini-bar and robes.

FACILITIES/SERVICES: Spa, fitness center, concierge, child care services, dry cleaning and shops.

BUSINESS SERVICES: On-site Business Center and secretarial services available.

DINING: "Splashes" serves a Mediterranean-inspired menu. Guests can enjoy indoor or patio dining with spectacular sunset views.

MEETINGS: Total Meeting Rooms: 13 Total Sq. Ft.: 10,000 / Sq. M.: 931

RATES: USD 295.00 to 1,100.00; Corporate, Group, Package rates.

Mr. Blaise Bartell, General Manager

1555 South Coast Highway
Laguna Beach, California 92651, USA
Tel: +1 949 497 4477
Fax: +1 949 494 7653
Email: surfandsandresort@jcresorts.com
www.jcresorts.com

This intimate, Mediterranean-style paradise offers informal luxury with a soft pastel scheme, travertine marble baths, plantation shutters and spectacular ocean views. Rolling surf and Pacific sunsets set the stage for relaxation and romance. Situated along 500 feet (152 meters) of white sand beach midway between Los Angeles and San Diego, directly on Laguna Beach. John Wayne Orange County Airport: 12 miles/19 km, 20 minutes.

Worldwide Reservations
www.preferredhotels.com
+800 323 7500 USA/Canada
+00 800 3237 5001 Europe (UIFN)
Other areas: See page 204

27

THE CARNEROS INN

The Carneros Inn is located amongst the rolling hills of the Mayacamas Range in the heart of the Carneros region. An official American viticultural district, the natural boundaries of the bay, mountain ranges, elevations and river combine to create a distinctive micro-destination that is rich in agriculture. The Inn accords a tranquil setting offering individual cottages with simplistic architectural lines, modern technology and contemporary décor. Napa is just 5 miles and Sonoma only 10 miles from the Inn. San Francisco Int'l, Oakland Airports: 50 miles/ 78km, 60 minutes. Sacramento Airport: 90 miles/ 145km, 90 minutes.

Worldwide Reservations
www.preferredhotels.com
+800 323 7500 USA/Canada
+00 800 3237 5001 Europe (UIFN)
Other areas: See page 204

ACCOMMODATIONS: 86 total cottages, including 10 suites, each a private oasis with decks and gardens. Fireplaces, alfresco showers, soaking tubs, high-speed Internet, flat-screen televisions, DVD/CD player and daily Vintner's breakfast.

FACILITIES/SERVICES: Spa with indoor and outdoor treatments overlooking the wine region. Cottage services bring the spa to your door. Pool, hot pool, sauna, steam rooms and fitness center. Concierge, afternoon beverage service and cottage dining.

BUSINESS SERVICES: Services available.

DINING: The "Boonfly Café," named after the Carneros pioneer of the 1800s, offers a casual gathering place for guests and locals. The food is rustic and inspired by the region's agriculture. Boxed lunches and picnics available for those going off to the vineyards.

MEETINGS: Total Meeting Rooms: 5 Total Sq. Ft.: 5,700 / Sq. M.: 550

RATES: USD 375.00 to 1,200.00; Corporate, Group, Package rates.

Mr. Michael B. Hoffmann, Managing Director

4048 Sonoma Highway
Napa, California 94559, USA
Tel: +1 707 299 4900
Fax: +1 707 299 4950
Email: reservations@
TheCarnerosInn.com
www.TheCarnerosInn.com

THE BALBOA BAY CLUB & RESORT

ACCOMMODATIONS: 136 total guestrooms, including 10 suites, boast a residential flair, each with patio, marble and granite bathrooms with sunken tubs, and feather-top beds with crisp white duvets.

FACILITIES/SERVICES: Spa, pool, concierge, shoe shine, fitness center, child care services, salon, dry cleaning and shops. Yachting, sailing and boating.

BUSINESS SERVICES: Full-service Business Center.

DINING: "The First Cabin" restaurant overlooks the yacht-filled harbor and alfresco terrace seating. California-inspired cuisine with a continental flair is offered for breakfast, lunch and dinner. A waterfront bar and entertainment lounge is the ideal spot for enjoying light fare, cocktails and live jazz nightly.

MEETINGS: Total Meeting Rooms: 10 Total Sq. Ft.: 15,464 / Sq. M.: 1,440

RATES: USD $295 to $3,500; Corporate, Group, Package rates.

Mr. Henry Schielein,
President & Chief Operating Officer

1221 West Coast Highway
Newport Beach, California 92663, USA
Tel: +1 949 645 5000
Fax: +1 949 630 4215
Email: reservations@balboabayclub.com
www.balboabayclub.com

The Balboa Bay Club & Resort, in the heart of Newport Beach on California's Riviera, is set against a stunning backdrop of sleek million-dollar yachts and spectacular bay views. The luxury resort is the only full-service waterfront hotel in Newport Beach and shares 15 prime bay-front acres with the historic Balboa Bay Club. Centrally located near Newport Beach's Fashion Island and Balboa Peninsula. John Wayne Airport: 8 miles/13 km, 15 minutes.

Newport Beach, California, USA

Worldwide Reservations
www.preferredhotels.com
+800 323 7500   USA/Canada
+00 800 3237 5001   Europe (UIFN)
Other areas: See page 204

29

MIRAMONTE RESORT, INDIAN WELLS

Miramonte is an intimate Tuscan-style retreat with curved archways and impressive stonework. Nestled in the foothills of the Santa Rosa Mountains on 11 acres (5 hectares) of lushly landscaped gardens, this intimate oasis offers attentive service while immersing guests in an inviting and tranquil old-world atmosphere. Located in the heart of Indian Wells, only minutes from the boutiques, restaurants and galleries of El Paseo. Palm Springs Airport: 10 miles/ 16 km, 20 minutes.

ACCOMMODATIONS: 215 total guestrooms, including 23 suites, each with three phones, data port, voice mail, newspaper, safe, mini-bar, robes and VCR on request.

FACILITIES/SERVICES: Spa, fitness center, concierge, child care services, dry cleaning, shoe shine and gift shop.

BUSINESS SERVICES: Business services available seven days a week.

DINING: "Brissago" offers unique Northern Italian cuisine in an elegant bistro setting.

MEETINGS: Total Meeting Rooms: 13 Total Sq. Ft.: 12,500 / Sq. M.: 1,161

RATES: USD 129.00 to 1,500.00; Corporate, Group, Package rates.

Mr. Elie G. Zod, General Manager

45000 Indian Wells Lane
Palm Springs/Indian Wells,
California 92210, USA
Tel: +1 760 341 2200
Fax: +1 760 568 0541
Email: miramonte.info@
miramonteresort.com
www.miramonteresort.com

Worldwide Reservations

www.preferredhotels.com

+800 323 7500 USA/Canada

+00 800 3237 5001 Europe (UIFN)

Other areas: See page 204

San Diego, California, USA

ACCOMMODATIONS: 287 total guestrooms, including 13 suites, each with data port, voice mail, safe, mini-bar, hair dryer and high-speed Internet access on request.

FACILITIES/SERVICES: 18-hole championship and 27-hole executive golf courses and pro shops, tennis courts, pools, fitness center, spa, bike rental, concierge, dry cleaning and extensive children's programs.

BUSINESS SERVICES: On-site Business Center and secretarial services available.

DINING: Offering upscale French cuisine in the top-rated "El Bizcocho" dining room, and southern European cuisine in the "Veranda Grill."

MEETINGS: Total Meeting Rooms: 15 Total Sq. Ft.: 15,000 / Sq. M.: 1,396

RATES: USD 259.00 to 1,500.00; Corporate, Group, Package rates.

Mr. Bob Peckenpaugh,
General Manager

17550 Bernardo Oaks Drive
San Diego, California 92128, USA
Tel: +1 858 675 8500
Fax: +1 858 675 8501
Email: ranchobernardoinn@
jcresorts.com
www.jcresorts.com

A sophisticated California mission-style resort, featuring golf, tennis and a full-service spa. Reminiscent of a country estate with lush California landscaping, and set against the backdrop of the San Pasquel Mountains, the Inn has a gracious and unpretentious style with genuine warmth, affording guests total relaxation. Located in San Diego North, with access to a full range of attractions. San Diego Int'l. Airport: 28 miles/45 km, 30 minutes.

Worldwide Reservations
www.preferredhotels.com
+800 323 7500 USA/Canada
+00 800 3237 5001 Europe (UIFN)
Other areas: See page 204

LA VALENCIA HOTEL

Intimate and charming, La Valencia Hotel has been the place to stay in La Jolla since opening in 1926. Just steps from the Pacific, it is fondly known as "the Jewel of La Jolla." On the Pacific Ocean in picturesque La Jolla. San Diego Int'l. Airport: 12 miles/19 km, 20 minutes.

ACCOMMODATIONS: 116 total guestrooms, including 17 suites, each with two multi-line phones, data port, voice mail, VCR, safe, mini-bar, robes, hair dryer, iron & board and newspaper.

FACILITIES/SERVICES: Pool, whirlpool, fitness center, spa services, concierge, dry cleaning and shoe shine.

BUSINESS SERVICES: Business, secretarial and translating services on request.

DINING: "The Sky Room" offers elegant California cuisine, "Whaling Bar & Grill" offers tableside service in a pub-like atmosphere and "Mediterranean Room" offers casual dining both indoors and on the Ocean View Terrace.

MEETINGS: Total Meeting Rooms: 3 Total Sq. Ft.: 5,000 / Sq. M.: 466

RATES: USD 300.00 to 3,500.00; Corporate, Group, Package rates.

Mr. Michael J. Ullman, General Manager

1132 Prospect Street
La Jolla, California 92037, USA
Tel: +1 858 454 0771
Fax: +1 858 456 3921
Email: info@lavalencia.com
www.lavalencia.com

Worldwide Reservations
www.preferredhotels.com
+800 323 7500 USA/Canada
+00 800 3237 5001 Europe (UIFN)
Other areas: See page 204

THE HUNTINGTON HOTEL & NOB HILL SPA

ACCOMMODATIONS: 135 total guestrooms, including 35 suites, each with mini-bar, safe, multi-line phones, data port, voice mail, fax machine and complimentary DSL access. VCR available on request.

FACILITIES/SERVICES: The Nob Hill Spa, overlooking the glorious San Francisco skyline, includes an indoor pool, a Jacuzzi, saunas and steam rooms, couple's massage room, massage, facial, nail and body treatments. Complimentary tea or sherry service, chauffeured sedan, dry cleaning, child care services, shoe shine, concierge and health club.

BUSINESS SERVICES: New on-site, full-service Business Center.

DINING: The "Big 4 Restaurant" for fine dining features contemporary American cuisine.

MEETINGS: Total Meeting Rooms: 4 Total Sq. Ft.: 1,800 / Sq. M.: 168

RATES: USD 295.00 to 1,130.00; Corporate, Group, Package rates.

Ms. Gail R. Isono, General Manager

  @

1075 California Street
San Francisco, California 94108, USA
Tel: +1 415 474 5400
Fax: +1 415 474 6227
Email: reservations@
huntingtonhotel.com
www.huntingtonhotel.com

The famed cable cars stop at the front doors of this elegant and intimate landmark, perched atop prestigious Nob Hill. Located off the lobby is the one-of-a-kind Nob Hill Spa, which combines the Japanese, Chinese, Italian and Victorian influences found in the architecture and people of San Francisco. At California and Taylor streets, four blocks from Union Square and the Theater District. San Francisco Int'l. Airport: 15 miles/24 km, 30 minutes.

Worldwide Reservations
www.preferredhotels.com
+800 323 7500 USA/Canada
+00 800 3237 5001 Europe (UIFN)
Other areas: See page 204

33

HOTEL VALENCIA SANTANA ROW

This new hotel, which opened in June 2003, evokes the feeling of a grand Tuscan palazzo that has weathered the ages. The hotel features an expansive open-air courtyard and rooftop wine terrace with open-pit fire that has breathtaking sunset views over the Santa Cruz Mountains. Located 3 miles/4 kms west of downtown San Jose in the heart of Santana Row, with shopping, dining, cinemas and residences. San Jose Int'l. Airport is a 10-minute drive and San Francisco Int'l. Airport is a 40-minute drive.

ACCOMMODATIONS: 213 total guestrooms, including 16 suites, each with custom-made bed, "Lather" bath amenities, bathrobes and mini bar; high-speed Internet access at desk and bedside; two dual-line speakerphones, one cordless; voice, data and video network infrastructure available.

FACILITIES/SERVICES: Outdoor heated pool with sundeck overlooking Santana Row, whirlpool, fitness center, spa, concierge, laundry and valet, shoe shine and children's program.

BUSINESS SERVICES: Full-service Business Center providing wireless Internet access.

DINING: "Citrus" features steak and chop menu all day. "V bar" flows into open-air courtyard and overlooks Santana Row. "Cielo" wine terrace features fire grottos and spectacular sunset views.

MEETINGS: Total Meeting Rooms: 5 Total Sq. Ft.: 3,804 / Sq. M.: 354

RATES: USD 139.00 to 319.00; Corporate, Group, Package rates.

Mr. Martin Duane, General Manager

355 Santana Row
San Jose, California 95128, USA
Tel: +1 408 551 0010
Fax: +1 408 551 0550
Email: santanarow@valenciagroup.com
www.hotelvalencia.com

Worldwide Reservations
www.preferredhotels.com
+800 323 7500 USA/Canada
+00 800 3237 5001 Europe (UIFN)
Other areas: See page 204

VINEYARD CREEK HOTEL, SPA AND CONFERENCE CENTER

ACCOMMODATIONS: 155 total guestrooms, including 20 suites, each with complimentary T-1 high-speed Internet access, multi-line cordless phones, voice mail, refreshment center, safe, down comforters, aromatherapy, newspapers, robes, fresh flowers, turndown tea service and in-room French-press coffee service available.

FACILITIES/SERVICES: Fully equipped spa with health and fitness center, outdoor pool and 24-hour concierge.

BUSINESS SERVICES: Secretarial services available.

DINING: "Seafood Brasserie," Sonoma County's finest French seafood cuisine restaurant, offers the best of local fare and serves California's finest wines from nearby wineries. 24-hour room service also available.

MEETINGS: Total Meeting Rooms: 15 Total Sq. Ft.: 41,000 / Sq. M.: 3,809. 21,000 Sq. Ft. conference space and 20,000 Sq. Ft. of outdoor event space.

RATES: USD 149.00 to 249.00; Suites 249.00 to 599.00; Corporate, Group, Package rates.

Mr. Brad Calkins, General Manager

170 Railroad Road
Santa Rosa, California 95401, USA
Tel: +1 707 636 7100
Fax: +1 707 636 7277
Email: info@vineyardcreek.com
www.vineyardcreek.com

The Vineyard Creek Hotel is a Mediterranean building centered around two large courtyards. The grounds are lushly landscaped, creating a secluded oasis within the city. The rooms are elegant and classic in design. In the heart of California's famed Wine Country and adjacent to historic Railroad Square, which features a collection of antique shops, gift shops and restaurants. Recently awarded AAA Four Diamond award. The hotel adjoins Santa Rosa Creek, with its landscaped walking and bike trails. San Francisco Int'l. Airport: 55 miles/88 km, 90 minutes.

Worldwide Reservations
www.preferredhotels.com
+800 323 7500 USA/Canada
+00 800 3237 5001 Europe (UIFN)
Other areas: See page 204

THE PINES LODGE

ACCOMMODATIONS: 68 total guestrooms, including 8 penthouse condominiums and townhouses, each with two phones, data port, voice mail, VCR, robes, refrigerator and coffee maker.

FACILITIES/SERVICES: Snow skiing, year-round ice skating, horse-back riding, hot air ballooning, snow-mobiling, fishing, golf, river rafting, hiking, fitness center, tennis, child care services, dry cleaning and concierge.

BUSINESS SERVICES: High-speed Internet terminals in all guest-rooms. Personalized secretarial and guest services.

DINING: The Pines Lodge's "Grouse Mountain Grill" features bold, creative regional American cuisine and AAA Four Diamond Award-winning service.

MEETINGS: Total Meeting Rooms: 6 Total Sq. Ft.: 3,145 / Sq. M.: 293

RATES: USD from 120.00; Corporate, Group, Package rates.

Mr. Steven Rose, General Manager

141 Scott Hill Road
Beaver Creek, Colorado 81620, USA
Tel: +1 970 845 7900
Fax: +1 970 845 7809
Email: vbcrp@vailresorts.com
www.rockresorts.com

Beaver Creek's hillside boutique resort hotel, this intimate ski-in/ski-out lodge upholds Laurance Rockefeller's founding vision of extraordinary accommodations in stunning settings. Natural rustic pine, heavy tapestries and fresh mountain wildflowers complement this RockResort, nestled among groves of aspen and pine trees with magnificent views. Relax after a full day of skiing or 18 holes of golf in this tranquil setting. Woven into the majestic setting of Beaver Creek, Colorado. Denver Int'l. Airport: 110 miles/177 km, 2 hours. Eagle County Airport: 30 miles/48 km, 20 minutes.

Worldwide Reservations
www.preferredhotels.com
+800 323 7500 USA/Canada
+00 800 3237 5001 Europe (UIFN)
Other areas: See page 204

THE EXCLUSIVE URBAN ESCAPE —
PREFERRED CITY BREAKS!

For your next urban escape, put Preferred to the test! Receive free parking and breakfast or a $100 Spa Credit with the *Preferred City Breaks* package from January 1–December 31, 2004. Challenge our top concierges to secure seats at the hottest show in town or to reserve a table at that chic new bistro. Also, be sure to leave enough room in your bags to accommodate the spoils of a world-class shopping spree!

For more information and to book a *Preferred City Breaks* package, please visit our Web site at www.preferredhotels.com/offers, contact your travel professional or call 1 800 323 7500.

ST. JULIEN HOTEL & SPA

ACCOMMODATIONS: 200 total guestrooms, including 12 suites, each with multi-line phones, data port, voice mail, safe, mini-bar, robes and hair dryer.

FACILITIES/SERVICES: Spa, concierge, fitness center and salon.

BUSINESS SERVICES: On-site Business Center.

DINING: The restaurant features American cuisine. A light menu is also available in the bar and on the terraces.

MEETINGS: Total Meeting Rooms: 9 Total Sq. Ft.: 10,500 / Sq. M.: 978

RATES: USD 195.00 to 350.00; Corporate, Group, Package rates.

Mr. Bruce Porcelli, Property Contact

---

900 Walnut Street
Boulder, Colorado 80302, USA
Tel: +1 720 406 9696
Fax: +1 720 406 9668
Email: stjulienhotel@aol.com
www.stjulien.com

The architecture uses local materials such as granite, sandstone and slate, and public areas and guestrooms have a timeless elegance with contemporary flair. Situated downtown with views of the Flatiron Mountains, the hotel is within walking distance of shops and restaurants. Guests will experience uncompromised service in an intimate and inviting atmosphere. The St. Julien Hotel & Spa is located in historic downtown Boulder, Colorado, and is within walking distance of the University of Colorado campus. Denver Int'l. 45 miles/72 km, 60 minutes. Shuttle service available.

Worldwide Reservations
www.preferredhotels.com
+800 323 7500   USA/Canada
+00 800 3237 5001   Europe (UIFN)
Other areas: See page 204

THE BROADMOOR

ACCOMMODATIONS: 700 total guestrooms, including 107 suites, each with two multi-line phones, data port, high-speed Internet access, voice mail, newspaper, safe, mini-bar, robes and CD players.

FACILITIES/SERVICES: World-renowned spa, three golf courses, fitness center, three swimming pools, tennis, child care services, dry cleaning, shoe shine, salon, florist, concierge and shops.

BUSINESS SERVICES: On-site Business Center, secretarial and translating services available. High-speed Internet access available in-room.

DINING: With 10 different restaurants and lounges featuring a variety of delectable cuisines, The Broadmoor can satisfy every dining preference and palate.

MEETINGS: Total Meeting Rooms: 52 Total Sq. Ft.: 114,000 / Sq. M.: 10,613

RATES: USD 230.00 to 3,170.00; Corporate, Group, Package rates.

Mr. Steve Bartolin,
President & CEO

1 Lake Avenue
Colorado Springs, Colorado 80906,
USA
Tel: +1 719 634 7711
Fax: +1 719 577 5700
Email: sales@broadmoor.com
www.broadmoor.com

Originally opened in 1918 and renovated in 2002, this "Grand Dame of the Rockies" continues to shine brightly as one of the world's premier resorts. On 3,000 acres (1,214 hectares) at the foot of the Colorado Rockies, this invigorating and luxurious mountain retreat offers a legacy of elegance, impeccable service and exquisite cuisine. Minutes from downtown Colorado Springs, Pikes Peak Cog Railway, Garden of the Gods and Cheyenne Mountain Zoo. Colorado Springs Airport: 12 miles/19 km, 20 minutes. Just 90 minutes south of Denver Int'l. Airport and flights worldwide.

Worldwide Reservations
www.preferredhotels.com
+800 323 7500   USA/Canada
+00 800 3237 5001   Europe (UIFN)
Other areas: See page 204

You say jump...
we ask how high?

At Preferred hotels and resorts, our mantra is service.
From bellhop to housekeeper, concierge to valet,
we look forward to being put through our paces.

PREFERRED
HOTELS & RESORTS
WORLD WIDE

THE BROWN PALACE HOTEL

ACCOMMODATIONS: 230 total guestrooms, including 25 suites, each with two multi-line phones, data port, newspaper, robes, complimentary high-speed Internet access and private voice mail.

FACILITIES/SERVICES: Fitness center, full-service concierge, dry cleaning and florist.

BUSINESS SERVICES: On-site Business Center, secretarial and translating services available.

DINING: Choice of three restaurants: Enjoy fine dining in "Palace Arms;" breakfast, lunch or Dom Perignon Sunday brunch in "Ellyngton's;" casual dining with a piano bar in the local favorite, "Ship Tavern;" spirits and cigars in "Churchill Bar."

MEETINGS: Total Meeting Rooms: 14 Total Sq. Ft.: 15,000 / Sq. M.: 1,396

RATES: USD 220.00 to 1,200.00; Corporate, Group, Package rates.

Mr. Armel Santens,
Managing Director

321 Seventeenth Street
Denver, Colorado 80202, USA
Tel: +1 303 297 3111
Fax: +1 303 312 5900
Email: marketing@brownpalace.com
www.brownpalace.com

For more than a century, the Italian Renaissance style of this historic landmark has delighted guests with its onyx walls, terrazzo floors and gold-leaf highlights. Once inside and away from the bustle of the city, guests can relax while enjoying afternoon tea in the luxurious atrium lobby, complete with soothing sounds of a harp or piano. Located in the heart of downtown, an easy walk to Denver's museums, performing arts venues and major league sporting events. Denver Int'l. Airport: 25 miles/40 km, 40 minutes.

ACCOMMODATIONS: 152 total guestrooms, including 14 suites, each with two multi-line phones, data port, voice mail, newspaper, iron & board, hair dryer and robes. VCR and fax available on request.

FACILITIES/SERVICES: World-class skiing, ice skating, snowmobiling, snowshoeing, cross-country skiing and sleigh rides in winter; 36 holes of championship golf, horseback riding, mountain biking, rafting, hiking, fly-fishing and tennis in summer.

BUSINESS SERVICES: Adjacent to the 100,000-square-foot Keystone Convention Center, the largest resort meeting facility west of the Mississippi. Business Center, A/V services and satellite teleconferencing.

DINING: Keystone Resort offers more than 30 dining options, including two AAA Four Diamond Award winning restaurants, "The Keystone Ranch" and "Alpenglow Stube," as well as "Champeaux," lakeside.

MEETINGS: Total Meeting Rooms: 50 Total Sq. Ft.: 100,000 / Sq. M.: 9,310

RATES: USD 107.00 to 334.00; Group, Package rates.

Mr. John Luckett, General Manager

22010 U.S. Highway 6
Keystone, Colorado 80435, USA
Tel: +1 970 496 2316
Fax: +1 970 496 4215
Email: keystoneinfo@vailresorts.com
www.rockresorts.com

Lakeside, in a charming alpine-style village, Keystone Lodge offers guests myriad activities and gracious service. Faithful to Laurance Rockefeller's original vision, this luxurious RockResort both reflects and enhances its spectacular setting. Surrounded by the Rockies and thousands of acres of National Forest, Keystone Lodge is located in the heart of Keystone Resort, a premier year-round destination. Denver Int'l. Airport: 90 miles/120 km, 90 minutes.

Worldwide Reservations
www.preferredhotels.com
+800 323 7500 USA/Canada
+00 800 3237 5001 Europe (UIFN)
Other areas: See page 204

ACCOMMODATIONS: 165 total guestrooms, including 49 suites, each with dual-line phone, data port, voice mail, DVD/VCR, newspaper and robes.

FACILITIES/SERVICES: Alpine and cross-country skiing, golf, white-water rafting, kayaking, fly-fishing, hot air ballooning, hiking, biking, fitness center, child care services, dry cleaning, concierge and shops.

BUSINESS SERVICES: On-site business services, secretarial and translating services available.

DINING: Signature dining in the "Wildflower," Vail's only 2003 Mobil Four Star Award-winning restaurant, offers creative American cuisine; and "Cucina Rustica" features skier's buffets and Italian-inspired fare. "Mickey's Piano Bar" is a Vail tradition.

MEETINGS: Total Meeting Rooms: 7 Total Sq. Ft.: 9,269 / Sq. M.: 863

RATES: USD from 150.00; Corporate, Group, Package rates.

Mr. Wolfgang Triebnig, General Manager

174 East Gore Creek Drive
Vail, Colorado 81657, USA
Tel: +1 970 476 5011
Fax: +1 970 476 7425
Email: reservations@lodgeatvail.com
www.rockresorts.com

True to Laurance Rockefeller's founding vision, this charming European-style RockResort combines the rustic nature of Colorado with the elegance and charm of an old-world inn. The Lodge, Vail's only 2003 Mobil Four Star Award–winning hotel, is located in the heart of Vail Village, just steps from world-class skiing, shopping and dining. Guests will enjoy relaxed luxury with the warmth of Western hospitality in the perfect mountain location. Denver Int'l. Airport: 120 miles/193 km, 120 minutes. Vail/Eagle County Airport: 35 miles/56 km, 40 minutes.

Worldwide Reservations
www.preferredhotels.com
+800 323 7500   USA/Canada
+00 800 3237 5001   Europe (UIFN)
Other areas: See page 204

HOTEL DU PONT

Long known for its old-world elegance, this 12-story Italian Renaissance hotel houses many original paintings, including three generations of Wyeths. Breathtaking scenery and a wealth of historical attractions are a short drive from the hotel's door. In downtown Wilmington, close to the historic Winterthur Museum and Gardens. Philadelphia Int'l. Airport: 19 miles/ 31 km, 25 minutes.

ACCOMMODATIONS: 217 total guestrooms, including 12 suites, each with voice mail in three languages, data port, newspaper, mini-bars, robes, TV entertainment center and in-room safe.

FACILITIES/SERVICES: 1,200-seat theater, fitness club with sauna, gift shop, shoe shine, hair salon and concierge.

BUSINESS SERVICES: On-site Business Center available.

DINING: Historic "Green Room" serving breakfast, lunch and dinner. Afternoon tea and cocktails served in the "Lobby Lounge."

MEETINGS: Total Meeting Rooms: 32 Total Sq. Ft.: 30,000 / Sq. M.: 2,793

RATES: USD 179.00 to 650.00; Corporate, Group, Package rates.

Mr. Charles E. Henning, General Manager

11th and Market Streets
Wilmington, Delaware 19801, USA
Tel: +1 302 594 3100
Fax: +1 302 594 3108
Email: hotel.dupont@usa.dupont.com
www.hoteldupont.com

Worldwide Reservations
www.preferredhotels.com
+800 323 7500 USA/Canada
+00 800 3237 5001 Europe (UIFN)
Other areas: See page 204

HOTEL GEORGE

ACCOMMODATIONS: 139 total guestrooms, including 3 suites, each featuring 300-thread count linens, multi-line cordless phones, data port, voice mail, newspaper, safe, mini-bar, CD/stereo clock radio with nature sounds, iron & board, umbrella and robes, high-speed Internet access; some rooms equipped with fax machines.

FACILITIES/SERVICES:
Complimentary 24-hour fitness center, steam room, concierge, child care services, dry cleaning, shoe shine and billiards room.

BUSINESS SERVICES: Secretarial services. All meeting rooms equipped with high-speed Internet access.

DINING: Dine in the George's award-winning restaurant "Bistro Bis." Chef Jeffrey Buben's celebrated menu features creative interpretations of classic French bistro fare.

MEETINGS: Total Meeting Rooms: 4 Total Sq. Ft.: 2,488 / Sq. M.: 232

RATES: USD 250.00 to 900.00; Corporate, Group, Package rates.

Ms. Sholeh Kia, General Manager

@

15 E Street, NW
Washington, D.C. 20001, USA
Tel: +1 202 347 4200
Fax: +1 202 347 4213
Email: rooms@hotelgeorge.com
www.hotelgeorge.com

Providing guests with an intimate and contemporary setting and located at the nucleus of the Washington government, culture and business district, the George achieves a perfect balance between personalized service and a sophisticated hotel experience. Situated just west of North Capitol Street, one block from Union Station, Metro and walking distance to the U.S. Capitol, Smithsonian Institution and Supreme Court. Reagan Nat'l. Airport: 4 miles/6 km. Dulles Int'l. Airport: 25 miles/38 km.

Worldwide Reservations
www.preferredhotels.com
+800 323 7500 USA/Canada
+00 800 3237 5001 Europe (UIFN)
Other areas: See page 204

WASHINGTON TERRACE HOTEL

Highlighted by three beautifully landscaped terraces, the Washington Terrace Hotel is a serene oasis in the heart of a vibrant city. Guests will enjoy a sophisticated blend of boutique style and traditional touches as well as exceptional hospitality. Near Scott Circle in northwest Washington, six blocks from the White House. Three blocks from the Connecticut Avenue and K Street business and shopping districts. Near museums, monuments and National Zoo. Three blocks from Metro stations at Dupont Circle and McPherson Square. Reagan Nat'l. Airport: 3 miles/4.8 km, 10 minutes.

ACCOMMODATIONS: 220 total guestrooms, including 39 suites, each with cordless phone, data port, high-speed Internet access, radio/CD player, mini-bar, coffee maker and in-room safe that holds a laptop. Corporate-level floors.

FACILITIES/SERVICES: Fitness center, laundry and dry cleaning.

BUSINESS SERVICES: On-site Business Center with concierge.

DINING: "15 ria," a bistro-style restaurant with a retro-style bar, features fresh local and regional products prepared in a straightforward fashion. Seasonal outdoor dining. Weekend brunch available.

MEETINGS: Total Meeting Rooms: 9 Total Sq. Ft.: 6,700 / Sq. M.: 624

RATES: USD 139.00 to 750.00; Corporate, Group, Package rates.

Mr. John O'Sullivan, General Manager

1515 Rhode Island Avenue, NW
Washington, D.C. 20005, USA
Tel: +1 202 232 7000
Fax: +1 202 332 8436
Email: reservations@
washingtonterracehotel.com
www.washingtonterracehotel.com

Worldwide Reservations
www.preferredhotels.com
+800 323 7500 USA/Canada
+00 800 3237 5001 Europe (UIFN)
Other areas: See page 204

In Good Hands

Let the pampering begin! From Portland to Paris, Mexico to Morocco, we invite you to experience the plush-pile luxury of a Preferred hotel or resort.

AMELIA ISLAND PLANTATION INN

The Amelia Island Plantation Inn offers unique, spacious hotel rooms, each equipped with private balconies overlooking the ocean. Nestled between the wide, uncrowded beaches of the Atlantic and the tidal marshes of the Intracoastal, Amelia Island Plantation is a place where guests can relax in the tranquility of nature. Located on Amelia Island in Northeast Florida, adjacent to historic Fernandina Beach. Jacksonville Int'l. Airport: 29 miles/47 km, 40 minutes.

ACCOMMODATIONS: 249 total guestrooms, including 3 suites, each oceanfront room features two multi-line phones, data port, voice mail, newspaper, safe, mini-bar, robes, hair dryer, video games, movies, in-room coffee maker with premium coffee, 318-thread-count Egyptian linens and spa amenities.

FACILITIES/SERVICES: 3.5 miles of beach, 54 holes of championship golf, spa and salon, concierge, shoe shine, health and fitness center, 23 clay tennis courts, dry cleaning, shopping, youth programs, child care services, nature tours and fishing.

BUSINESS SERVICES: Full-service Business Center, wireless Internet access.

DINING: Eight restaurants offer a variety of options from fine dining with contemporary regional cuisine to charmingly casual with the freshest seafood.

MEETINGS: Total Meeting Rooms: 29 Total Sq. Ft.: 49,000 / Sq. M.: 4,562

RATES: USD 181.00 to 341.00; Group, Package rates.

Mr. Walther Vliegen,
Vice President & General Manager

6800 First Coast Highway
Amelia Island, Florida 32034, USA
Tel: +1 904 261 6161
Fax: +1 904 277 5159
Email: reservations@aipfl.com
www.aipfl.com

Worldwide Reservations
www.preferredhotels.com
+800 323 7500 USA/Canada
+00 800 3237 5001 Europe (UIFN)
Other areas: See page 204

SANIBEL HARBOUR RESORT & SPA

ACCOMMODATIONS: 401 total guestrooms, including 69 suites and 52 two-bedroom condominiums, each with two multi-line phones, data port, voice mail, safe, mini-bar, newspaper, robes, hair dryer, coffee maker, high-speed Internet access, on-demand movies and private balconies. VCR available.

FACILITIES/SERVICES: Spa, fitness center, tennis, day cruises, marina, watercraft rentals, fishing pier, nature trails, children's program. The beaches of Sanibel and Captiva islands, the historic Edison Home and Ford Estate, theaters and art galleries are nearby.

BUSINESS SERVICES: Business Center.

DINING: Award-winning creations at "Chez le Bear"; steaks and seafood at "Courtside Steakhouse & Sports Bar"; healthy favorites at the "Promenade Café" or dinner cruises aboard the "Sanibel Harbour Princess."

MEETINGS: Total Meeting Rooms: 28 Total Sq. Ft.: 45,000 / Sq. M.: 4,190

RATES: USD 139.00 to 1,149.00; Corporate, Group, Package rates.

Mr. Brian Holly, Managing Director

17260 Harbour Pointe Drive
Fort Myers, Florida 33908, USA
Tel: +1 239 466 4000
Fax: +1 239 466 6050
Email: shrs@sanibel-resort.com
www.sanibel-resort.com

Nestled on a lush, tropical 85-acre peninsula with spectacular views of Sanibel and Captiva islands. Sanibel Harbour Resort & Spa features romantic "Old Florida" architecture and exquisite furnishings that combine to create a warm and inviting casually elegant style. Watch the rest of the world recede with the tide at this enchanting and relaxing seaside sanctuary. Just minutes from Sanibel and Captiva islands in an area rich in tradition. Southwest Florida Int'l. Airport (RSW) 19 miles/31 km, 35 minutes.

Worldwide Reservations
www.preferredhotels.com
+800 323 7500 USA/Canada
+00 800 3237 5001 Europe (UIFN)
Other areas: See page 204

THE LODGE & CLUB AT PONTE VEDRA BEACH

Framed by palm trees and sand dunes, this 10-acre (4-hectare) oceanfront resort sparkles with sophistication and elegance. The Mediterranean-inspired architecture creates the illusion of a charming seaside European village. The soothing sounds of the Atlantic surf set the mood for this warm and inviting atmosphere. Ponte Vedra Beach is a 20-minute drive from Jacksonville. Jacksonville Int'l. Airport: 35 miles/56 km, 40 minutes.

ACCOMMODATIONS: 66 total guestrooms, including 24 suites, each with coffee maker, Jacuzzi or Roman garden tub, data port, voice mail, newspaper, safe, mini-bar and robes. Some rooms with fireplace. VCR on request.

FACILITIES/SERVICES: Three heated swimming pools, spa, fitness center, concierge, valet parking, high tea daily, child care services, dry cleaning, shoe shine and shops.

BUSINESS SERVICES: On-site Business Center and secretarial services available.

DINING: Dining pleasures include: "The Innlet" for fine dining and "The Oasis" beachfront patio (seasonal).

MEETINGS: Total Meeting Rooms: 7 Total Sq. Ft.: 5,680 / Sq. M.: 529

RATES: USD 190.00 to 510.00; Corporate, Group, Package rates.

Mr. David Mariotti, General Manager

607 Ponte Vedra Boulevard
Ponte Vedra Beach, Florida 32082, USA
Tel: +1 904 273 9500
Fax: +1 904 273 0210
Email: reservations@pvresorts.com
www.pvresorts.com

Worldwide Reservations
www.preferredhotels.com
+800 323 7500 USA/Canada
+00 800 3237 5001 Europe (UIFN)
Other areas: See page 204

MARCO BEACH OCEAN RESORT®

ACCOMMODATIONS: 100 one- and two-bedroom suites, each with full kitchen, separate living room, private balcony, mini-bar, robes, Molton Brown products, marble baths with separate showers, 300-count linens, multi-line phones, digital movies/music, data port, voice mail, safe and newspaper.

FACILITIES/SERVICES: Spa, fitness center, concierge, full beach services, dry cleaning and valet parking. Golf and offshore/backwater fishing nearby.

BUSINESS SERVICES: On-site Business Center; executive conference rooms and secretarial services available.

DINING: "Sale e Pepe" transports guests to Italy with a native Italian menu, offering casual or fine dining, indoors or out under the stars. "Toulouse" is an intimate lounge resembling turn-of-the-century Paris. Pool and beach bar also available.

MEETINGS: Total Meeting Rooms: 4 Total Sq. Ft.: 4,740 / Sq. M.: 441

RATES: USD 199.00 to 859.00; Corporate, Group, Package rates.

Mr. Phillip Starling, Managing Director

Antiques and original artwork surround guests with old-world charm reminiscent of the Italian Renaissance. Situated along Marco Island's famous beaches, overlooking the Gulf of Mexico. Superb services and luxurious amenities ensure the ultimate retreat experience. On the Gulf of Mexico, a short drive to Naples. Naples Airport: 18 miles/29 km, 30 minutes. Southwest Florida Int'l. Airport: 51 miles/83 km, 45 minutes.

480 South Collier Boulevard
Marco Island, Florida 34145, USA
Tel: +1 239 393 1400
Fax: +1 239 393 1401
Email: mborreservations@gulfbay.com
www.marcoresort.com

Worldwide Reservations
www.preferredhotels.com
+800 323 7500 USA/Canada
+00 800 3237 5001 Europe (UIFN)
Other areas: See page 204

THE NATIONAL HOTEL

Envision the 1940s, an era of grace, style and Old Hollywood glamour, all embodied within a beachfront property in the heart of South Beach. This is The National Hotel. Exuding stylish sophistication, the hotel provides impeccable service and an unparalleled guest experience. With tropical gardens and a 60-meter pool, it's hard to believe that the lights of South Beach lie beyond the palm trees. Ideally located on the ocean in the heart of South Beach, steps from fashionable Ocean Drive and Lincoln Road.

ACCOMMODATIONS: 150 total guestrooms, including 8 suites. Guests may choose from 115 oceanfront or city-view rooms in the Main Tower; as well as THE TRIPLEX, the new three-floor penthouse suite. 39 newly refurbished Cabana rooms with private terraces also available.

FACILITIES/SERVICES: The longest pool in Miami Beach, water sports (nearby) and fitness room available.

BUSINESS SERVICES: Secretarial services and high-speed Internet connections in every room.

DINING: One of the best restaurants on South Beach, "Tamara" offers a French fusion menu. Dine under the famous mosaic or outside overlooking the hotel's garden and infinity pool. "Latitude 26", a beachfront bar, serves barbecue-style lunch daily. The chic "Deco Lounge" features various entertainers.

MEETINGS: Total Meeting Rooms: 4 Total Sq. Ft.: 2,195 / Sq. M.: 204

RATES: USD 270.00 to 3,000.00; Corporate, Group, Package rates.

Mr. Jeff Lehman, General Manager

1677 Collins Avenue
Miami Beach, Florida 33139, USA
Tel: +1 305 532 2311
Fax: +1 305 532 0844
Email: ksjanzon@nationalhotel.com
www.nationalhotel.com

Worldwide Reservations
www.preferredhotels.com
+800 323 7500 USA/Canada
+00 800 3237 5001 Europe (UIFN)
Other areas: See page 204

MAYFAIR HOUSE HOTEL

ACCOMMODATIONS: 179 suites, fully renovated in 2003, each featuring a Roman tub or Japanese wooden hot tub on the balcony, as well as two multi-line phones, data port, voice mail, CD player, VCR, bathroom TV, newspaper, mini-bar, robes and hair dryer.

FACILITIES/SERVICES: Rooftop pool, Jacuzzi, spa, health club privileges, concierge, dry cleaning, shoe shine, child care services, salon, florist and shops.

BUSINESS SERVICES: On-site Business Center, secretarial and translating services available.

DINING: "The Mayfair Grill" offers a delicious breakfast in an elegant décor of orchids and stained glass; "The Orchid Lounge & Restaurant" offers a selection of wines and a bistro menu.

MEETINGS: Total Meeting Rooms: 10 Total Sq. Ft.: 12,000 / Sq. M.: 1,117

RATES: USD 169.00 to 999.00; Corporate, Group, Package rates.

Mr. Jon Wubbena, General Manager

3000 Florida Avenue
Coconut Grove, Florida 33133, USA
Tel: +1 305 441 0000
Fax: +1 305 443 4812
Email: mail@mayfairhousehotel.com
www.mayfairhousehotel.com

A unique Art Nouveau–style hotel full of antique and contemporary treasures, the Mayfair House is the focal point of exciting Coconut Grove. Fragrant orchids, flowing spaces, rich stained glass and antique art create the perfect environment for fine dining and elegant functions both intimate in nature and grand in scale. Mayfair House is located in the center of a tropical bayside village with shopping, dining, museums, art galleries and entertainment. 10 minutes from downtown, the beach and golf. Miami Int'l. Airport: 7 miles/11 km, 10 minutes.

Worldwide Reservations
www.preferredhotels.com
+800 323 7500 USA/Canada
+00 800 3237 5001 Europe (UIFN)
Other areas: See page 204

THE PEABODY ORLANDO

This contemporary hotel is famous for its marble halls, cascading waterfalls, orchids, million-dollar art collection and its famous residents, The Peabody Ducks. Located in the heart of one of the most popular vacation lands, it offers an unparalleled blend of service and Southern elegance to ensure an unforgettable stay. Close to SeaWorld and Discovery Cove, Universal Orlando, Islands of Adventure, Millennium Mall, Festival Bay and Pointe Orlando, and across the street from the convention center. Orlando Int'l. Airport: 13 miles/21 km, 20 minutes.

ACCOMMODATIONS: 891 total guestrooms, including 57 suites, each with TV in bathroom, data port, voice mail, newspaper, in-room safe, hair dryer, robes and mini-bar; some rooms with CD player. VCR available on request.

FACILITIES/SERVICES: Fitness center, tennis, concierge, child care services, dry cleaning, shoe shine, salon, shops, massage therapy, golf services and fully stocked pro shop. Four lighted, hard-top tennis courts, swimming pool, children's pool, whirlpool, bar and cabana.

BUSINESS SERVICES: On-site executive Business Center, secretarial and translating services available.

DINING: "Capriccio Grill" offers classic grilled steaks, seafood and traditional Italian favorites; "Dux," seasonal haute global cuisine; "B-Line Diner," Californian cuisine.

MEETINGS: Total Meeting Rooms: 32 Total Sq. Ft.: 57,000 / Sq. M.: 5,307

RATES: USD 390.00 to 1,675.00; Corporate, Group, Package rates.

Mr. Alan Villaverde,
Vice President & General Manager

9801 International Drive
Orlando, Florida 32819, USA
Tel: +1 407 352 4000
Fax: +1 407 351 9177
Email: peabodyinfo@
peabodyorlando.com
www.peabodyorlando.com

Worldwide Reservations
www.preferredhotels.com
+800 323 7500 USA/Canada
+00 800 3237 5001 Europe (UIFN)
Other areas: See page 204

CELEBRATION HOTEL

Opened in 1999, this luxury boutique resort in the downtown lakefront community of Celebration features architecture and furnishings reminiscent of early 1900s Florida. Adjacent to Walt Disney World Resort, the resort is situated lakeside in the scenic town of Celebration. A charming, intimate resort that is close to the attractions yet a world away. Orlando Int'l. Airport: 17 miles/27 km, 20 minutes.

ACCOMMODATIONS: 115 total guestrooms, including 6 suites, each with three phones, data port, voice mail, newspaper, safe, hair dryer, make-up mirror, iron & board, and Lodgenet Nintendo.

FACILITIES/SERVICES: The Robert Trent Jones Jr. and Sr. –designed golf course, fitness center and day spa, concierge, shopping, salon, dry cleaning and shops. Day rental of bikes, scooters and neighborhood electric vehicles.

BUSINESS SERVICES: Secretarial services, translating services, facsimile and copier.

DINING: The award-winning "Plantation Room," Old Florida charm, New Florida taste. The lobby Piano Bar featuring signature Martinis overlooking the lake.

MEETINGS: Total Meeting Rooms: 5 Total Sq. Ft.: 5,000 / Sq. M.: 466

RATES: USD 175.00 to 425.00; Corporate, Group, Package rates.

Mr. Roger Ploum, General Manager

700 Bloom Street
Celebration, Florida 34747, USA
Tel: +1 407 566 6000
Fax: +1 407 566 6001
Email: reservations@
celebrationhotel.com
www.celebrationhotel.com

Worldwide Reservations

www.preferredhotels.com
+800 323 7500 USA/Canada
+00 800 3237 5001 Europe (UIFN)
Other areas: See page 204

THE CASA MONICA HOTEL

ACCOMMODATIONS: 138 total guestrooms, including 14 suites, each with three multi-line phones, data port, voice mail, newspaper, safe, robes and hair dryer. Refrigerators in some rooms.

FACILITIES/SERVICES: Serenata Beach Club, spa services, fitness center, concierge, shoe shine, child care services and shops. More than 20 golf courses nearby.

BUSINESS SERVICES: Complimentary Business Center and secretarial services.

DINING: "95 Cordova," St. Augustine's only Four Star restaurant, serves the freshest, most unique dishes in Florida. The award-winning restaurant is popular with locals and hotel guests alike. Private wine rooms available for special occasions. "Cafe Cordova," a gourmet market, serves cappuccino, sandwiches, pastries and desserts.

MEETINGS: Total Meeting Rooms: 8 Total Sq. Ft.: 15,000 / Sq. M.: 1,396

RATES: USD 129.00 to 999.00; Corporate, Group, Package rates.

Mr. Marcel Pitton, General Manager

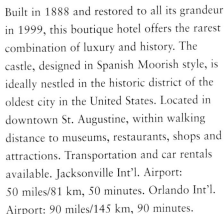

Built in 1888 and restored to all its grandeur in 1999, this boutique hotel offers the rarest combination of luxury and history. The castle, designed in Spanish Moorish style, is ideally nestled in the historic district of the oldest city in the United States. Located in downtown St. Augustine, within walking distance to museums, restaurants, shops and attractions. Transportation and car rentals available. Jacksonville Int'l. Airport: 50 miles/81 km, 50 minutes. Orlando Int'l. Airport: 90 miles/145 km, 90 minutes.

95 Cordova Street
St. Augustine, Florida 32084, USA
Tel: +1 904 827 1888
Fax: +1 904 819 6065
Email: info@casamonica.com
www.casamonica.com

Worldwide Reservations
www.preferredhotels.com
+800 323 7500 USA/Canada
+00 800 3237 5001 Europe (UIFN)
Other areas: See page 204

CHÂTEAU ÉLAN WINERY & RESORT

An elegant 16th-century-style French chateau and winery set on 3,500 acres (1,416 hectares) of rolling hills surrounded by lush vineyards. The French country estate setting enriched with Southern hospitality provides a unique resort experience with challenging golf, tennis, a spa and superb restaurants. Located just north of Atlanta, immediately off Interstate 85. Hartsfield Int'l. Airport: 50 miles/81 km, 50 minutes.

ACCOMMODATIONS: 290 total guestrooms, including 21 suites, each with three phones, data port, voice mail, newspaper, mini-bar, robes, hair dryer, sunken tub and walk-in shower. VCR available on request.

FACILITIES/SERVICES: Championship golf, European-style spa, four pools, seven tennis courts, equestrian center, performance driving school, winery tours and tastings, nature trails and Kids Club. Concierge, fitness center, child care services and dry cleaning.

BUSINESS SERVICES: Business Center and secretarial services.

DINING: Eight unique dining options, ranging from the wine-paired menus of "Le Clos" and the casual bistro fare at "Café Élan" to the health-inspired dishes of "Fleur-de-Lis."

MEETINGS: Total Meeting Rooms: 29 Total Sq. Ft.: 38,000 / Sq. M.: 3,538

RATES: USD 139.00 to 250.00; Corporate, Group, Package rates.

Mr. Henk Evers, President & CEO

100 Rue Charlemagne
Braselton, Georgia 30517, USA
Tel: +1 678 425 0900
Fax: +1 678 425 6000
Email: info@chateauelan.com
www.chateauelan.com

Worldwide Reservations

www.preferredhotels.com
+800 323 7500 USA/Canada
+00 800 3237 5001 Europe (UIFN)
Other areas: See page 204

MANSION ON FORSYTH PARK

Savannah, Georgia, USA

ACCOMMODATIONS: 126 total guestrooms and suites, including an exquisite 3-bedroom suite, each with soaker tub, three phones (two with multiple lines), data port, high-speed Internet access, voice mail, newspaper, CD player, safe, mini-bar, robes, hair dryer and luxury bedding.

FACILITIES/SERVICES: Spa, culinary school, concierge, fitness center, dry cleaning and shops. Historic Savannah tours available.

BUSINESS SERVICES: On-site Business Center and secretarial services available.

DINING: Located within a Historic 1888 mansion, "700 Drayton" offers contemporary American cuisine featuring fresh fish, prime cuts of steak, and daily market-inspired creations, all done with a Savannah flair. Six private dining rooms.

MEETINGS: Total Meeting Rooms: 6 Total Sq. Ft.: 7,000 / Sq. M.: 652

RATES: USD 195.00 and up; Corporate, Group, Package rates.

700 Drayton Street
Savannah, Georgia 31401, USA
Tel: +1 888 711 5114
Fax: +1 407 996 9998
Email: info@mansiononforsythpark.com
www.mansiononforsythpark.com

Savannah design is woven throughout this historic landmark. Located in the only planned renaissance city in America, the Mansion offers inviting accommodations, culinary experiences and spa services. Dramatic architecture, interiors and gardens create an extraordinary environment perfect for memorable getaways, meetings and events. Located in the historic district of Savannah, the Mansion on Forsyth Park is within walking distance to shopping, arts and antiques. Savannah Airport: 15 mi/ 24 km, 20 min.

Worldwide Reservations
www.preferredhotels.com
+800 323 7500 USA/Canada
+00 800 3237 5001 Europe (UIFN)
Other areas: See page 204

HALEKULANI

Lending elegance to the past, this modern hotel has retained much of its original 1920s charm and graciousness. Halekulani delivers understated luxury in an oasis of tranquility in the heart of Waikiki. Fine cuisine awaits guests at this luxurious paradise, where stellar service is standard. On Waikiki Beach, an easy walk to the Waikiki shopping district. Honolulu Int'l. Airport: 9 miles/ 14 km, 25 minutes. Hawaii Convention Center: 1 mile/2 km.

ACCOMMODATIONS: 455 total guestrooms, including 43 suites, each with balcony, three phones, fax modem service, complimentary local calls and wireless Internet service, fruit basket, newspaper, separate shower and soaking tub.

FACILITIES/SERVICES: Fitness center, concierge, child care services, dry cleaning, Business Center, hospitality suite, spa, florist and shops. Complimentary tickets to Oahu's cultural venues.

BUSINESS SERVICES: On-site Business Center; secretarial services, personal computers, Internet, fax and copy machines available.

DINING: Enjoy "La Mer" for exquisite neoclassic French cuisine, "Orchids" for contemporary seafood or "House Without A Key" for casual dining and nightly Hawaiian entertainment.

MEETINGS: Total Meeting Rooms: 5 Total Sq. Ft.: 8,454 / Sq. M.: 787

RATES: USD 325.00 to 4,500.00; Group, Package rates.

Mr. Fred Honda, General Manager

2199 Kalia Road
Honolulu, Hawaii 96815, USA
Tel: +1 808 923 2311
Fax: +1 808 926 8004
Email: reservations@halekulani.com
www.halekulani.com

Worldwide Reservations
www.preferredhotels.com
+800 323 7500   USA/Canada
+00 800 3237 5001   Europe (UIFN)
Other areas: See page 204

MAUNA LANI BAY HOTEL & BUNGALOWS

ACCOMMODATIONS: 350 total guestrooms including 10 suites and 5 private bungalows. Guestrooms feature private lanais, two phones, data port, voice mail, safe, private bar and robes.

FACILITIES/SERVICES: Mauna Lani Spa, sports and fitness club, lap pool, 36 holes of golf, tennis courts, ocean sports, children's camp, shops, florist and salon.

BUSINESS SERVICES: On-site services include wireless access, Internet, secretarial and translating services.

DINING: "Canoe House," Pacific Rim; "Bay Terrace," Mediterranean; "Gallery at the Golf Clubhouse," American fare; poolside dining at the "Ocean Grill," light dinners and sushi at the "Honu Bar."

MEETINGS: Total Meeting Rooms: 8 Total Sq. Ft.: 7,800 / Sq. M.: 726

RATES: USD 385.00 to 5,600.00; Corporate, Group, Package rates.

Mr. Kurt Matsumoto, Vice President

68-1400 Mauna Lani Drive
Kohala Coast, Hawaii 96743, USA
Tel: +1 808 885 6622
Fax: +1 808 885 1484
Email: reservations@maunalani.com
www.maunalani.com

Mauna Lani embodies the theme "Spirit of Place" with its acres of ancient fishponds and cultural activities. This luxurious oceanfront resort is an exquisite blend of understated elegance, superb cuisine, the new Mauna Lani Spa and world-class golf. Relax in an intimate surrounding enriched with Hawaiian aloha. Beachfront on the sunny Kohala Coast of the Big Island. Shopping and dining nearby and 20 minutes to the town of Waimea. Kona Int'l. Airport: 25 miles/40 km, 25 minutes.

THE COEUR d'ALENE RESORT

This world-class, full-service resort is situated on beautiful Lake Coeur d'Alene. The resort is the Northwest's premier golf, meeting and spa destination. Located in the heart of Idaho's pristine Northern Panhandle. Spokane Int'l. Airport: 25 miles/40 kms, 40 minutes.

ACCOMMODATIONS: 337 total guestrooms, including 10 suites, each with data port, high-speed Internet access, voice mail, newspaper, mini-bar, robes and hair dryer.

FACILITIES/SERVICES: Spa, concierge, shoe shine, fitness center, child care, salon, tennis, dry cleaning, florist and shops.

BUSINESS SERVICES: On-site Business Center, secretarial and translating services available.

DINING: Enjoy a number of excellent venues for your dining pleasure, including "Beverly's," "Dockside" and "Tito Macaroni's."

MEETINGS: Total Meeting Rooms: 27 Total Sq. Ft.: 23,000 / Sq. M.: 2,141

RATES: USD 109.00 to 399.00; Corporate, Group, Package rates.

Mr. William T. Reagan, General Manager

P.O. Box 7200, 115 S. 2nd Street
Coeur d'Alene, Idaho 83814, USA
Tel: +1 208 765 4000
Fax: +1 208 664 7276
Email: info@cdaresort.com
www.cdaresort.com

THE PENINSULA CHICAGO

ACCOMMODATIONS: 339 total guestrooms, including 83 suites, each with four multi-line phones, data port, voice mail, fax, wireless and DSL Internet access, mini-bar, televisions and robes in bathrooms. Suites with DVD, VCR and CD player.

FACILITIES/SERVICES: The Peninsula Spa, with city views, occupies the top two floors of the hotel. Fitness center, an 82-foot (7.6 square meters) swimming pool, Jacuzzi, treatment rooms and sundeck.

BUSINESS SERVICES: Business Center with offices and workstations.

DINING: For fine dining, "Avenues" has contemporary cuisine while "Shanghai Terrace" offers Asian dishes. "The Lobby" provides elegant all-day dining and tea. "The Bar" features a port and cigar collection. "Pierrot Gourmet" is reminiscent of a European cafe.

MEETINGS: Total Meeting Rooms: 8 Total Sq. Ft.: 17,000 / Sq. M.: 1,579

RATES: USD 425.00 to 5,500.00; Corporate, Group, Package rates.

Ms. Maria Razumich-Zec,
General Manager

108 East Superior Street
Chicago, Illinois 60611, USA
Tel: +1 312 337 2888
Fax: +1 312 751 2888
Email: pch@peninsula.com
www.peninsula.com

The classical limestone structure of The Peninsula Chicago reflects both the city's signature modern architecture and the elegance of neighboring buildings on North Michigan Avenue from the 1930s. Guests will enjoy luxurious accommodations, a spectacular glass-enclosed ballroom and The Terrace, which overlooks the "Magnificent Mile." Ideally located on North Michigan Avenue. O'Hare Int'l. Airport: 20 miles/32 km, 35 minutes.

Worldwide Reservations
www.preferredhotels.com
+800 323 7500   USA/Canada
+00 800 3237 5001   Europe (UIFN)
Other areas: See page 204

CANTERBURY HOTEL

An intimate, European-style hotel with Queen Anne and Chippendale-style furnishings, marble floors, imported cherry-wood and an elegant two-story atrium. Nestled in the heart of downtown Indianapolis, this historic landmark provides direct access to Circle Centre Mall via a skywalk on the mezzanine level. Located on the historic Illinois Street block next to the famous St. Elmo Steakhouse and near entertainment and dining facilities. Indianapolis Int'l. Airport: 8 miles/13 km, 15 minutes.

ACCOMMODATIONS: 99 total guestrooms, including 25 suites, each with complimentary WiFi (wireless high-speed Internet), three phones, data port, voice mail, newspaper, mini-bar, hair dryer and robes. CD player and VCR available on request.

FACILITIES/SERVICES: Complimentary passes to Gold's Gym, fitness room, concierge, dry cleaning, shoe shine, complimentary continental breakfast, and turndown service with chocolate truffles.

BUSINESS SERVICES: Secretarial and translating services available. Limo service available Monday-Friday, 7 to 8:30 a.m.

DINING: The award-winning "Restaurant at the Canterbury" features American and continental cuisine in an elegant, intimate setting. Afternoon tea is served daily at 4 p.m.

MEETINGS: Total Meeting Rooms: 5 Total Sq. Ft.: 2,673 / Sq. M.: 249

RATES: USD 175.00 to 2,250.00; Corporate, Group, Package rates.

Mrs. Letitia Moscrip, General Manager

123 South Illinois Street
Indianapolis, Indiana 46225, USA
Tel: +1 317 634 3000
Fax: +1 317 685 2519
Email: info@canterburyhotel.com
www.canterburyhotel.com

Worldwide Reservations
www.preferredhotels.com
+800 323 7500 USA/Canada
+00 800 3237 5001 Europe (UIFN)
Other areas: See page 204

The "Belle of New Orleans," built in 1907, is a completely restored, full-service hotel located in the heart of New Orleans. Guests can enjoy the elegance and history of New Orleans with each stay at Le Pavillon Hotel. Conveniently located near the Convention Center, Superdome, riverfront attractions and French Quarter. New Orleans Int'l. Airport: 13 miles/21 km, 30 minutes.

ACCOMMODATIONS: 226 total guestrooms, including 7 suites, each with three multi-line phones, data port, voice mail, newspaper, safe, mini-bar, robes and high-speed Internet access.

FACILITIES/SERVICES: Fitness center, concierge, child care services, dry cleaning, shoe shine, valet parking, heated pool and whirlpool.

BUSINESS SERVICES: High-speed Internet access available in meeting facilities and translating services available.

DINING: "Crystal Room" offers New Orleans cuisine, full breakfast, and a salad and pasta bar, along with full menu selections for lunch and dinner served nightly. "Gallery Lounge" offers light fare.

MEETINGS: Total Meeting Rooms: 8 Total Sq. Ft.: 9,063 / Sq. M.: 844

RATES: USD 230.00 to 3,000.00; Corporate, Group, Package rates.

Mr. Edward P. Morin, Managing Director

833 Poydras Street
New Orleans, Louisiana 70112, USA
Tel: +1 504 581 3111
Fax: +1 504 620 4130
Email: sales@lepavillon.com
www.lepavillon.com

Worldwide Reservations
www.preferredhotels.com
+800 323 7500 USA/Canada
+00 800 3237 5001 Europe (UIFN)
Other areas: See page 204

HARBOR COURT HOTEL

Decorated like the home of a well-traveled English explorer, Harbor Court offers European style and elegance with modern amenities. Guests can relax in luxurious surroundings and enjoy the pampering of an attentive staff. Overlooks the Inner Harbor within close proximity to the National Aquarium, Harborplace, Oriole Park and Ravens Stadium. Baltimore-Washington Int'l. Airport: 8 miles/13 km, 15 minutes.

ACCOMMODATIONS: 195 total guestrooms, including 21 suites, each with three multi-line phones, high-speed Internet access, voice mail, fax, CD player, newspaper, mini-bar, hair dryer and robes. VCR on request.

FACILITIES/SERVICES: Racquetball, yoga, fitness center, tennis, concierge, child care services, dry cleaning, shoe shine, massage and facial treatments, florist and parking garage.

BUSINESS SERVICES: On-site Business Center; secretarial and translating services and high-speed Internet access in meeting rooms available.

DINING: The award-winning "Hampton's" features seasonal American cuisine. "Café Brightons" offers casual dining. For cocktails, cigars and live jazz, try "Explorers Lounge."

MEETINGS: Total Meeting Rooms: 9 Total Sq. Ft.: 7,700 / Sq. M.: 717

RATES: USD 195.00 to 3,500.00; Corporate, Group, Package rates.

Mr. Werner R. Kunz,
Managing Director

550 Light Street
Baltimore, Maryland 21202, USA
Tel: +1 410 234 0550
Fax: +1 410 659 5925
Email: harbor@harborcourt.com
www.harborcourt.com

Worldwide Reservations
www.preferredhotels.com
+800 323 7500 USA/Canada
+00 800 3237 5001 Europe (UIFN)
Other areas: See page 204

THE ORCHARDS HOTEL

ACCOMMODATIONS: 49 total guestrooms, including 2 suites, some with fireplaces, each including two multi-line phones, data port, voice mail, VCR and robes.

FACILITIES/SERVICES: Fitness center, concierge, child care services, swimming pool, environmental chamber, bicycles and sauna.

BUSINESS SERVICES: Secretarial services available.

DINING: The award-winning "Yasmin's Restaurant" offers a sophisticated blend of international cuisine and classic New England favorites. "The Lounge" serves cocktails and light fare in a comfortable, relaxed atmosphere, and the "Courtyard" is a peaceful setting for alfresco dining. Visits to the Private Cellar may be made by appointment and are a special treat for wine lovers.

MEETINGS: Total Meeting Rooms: 4 Total Sq. Ft.: 2,700 / Sq. M.: 251

RATES: USD 215.00 to 325.00; Corporate, Group, Package rates.

Mr. Sayed M. Saleh,
President & Managing Director

  @

222 Adams Road
Williamstown, Massachusetts 01267, USA
Tel: +1 413 458 9611
Fax: +1 413 458 3273
Email: HotelAdmin@
OrchardsHotel.com
www.orchardshotel.com

This intimate hotel, built around a peaceful courtyard with a reflecting pool, fragrant blooms and stunning statuary, surrounds you with comfort. Nestled in the Berkshire Mountains, this hotel offers a tranquil refuge in America's premier cultural resort. Experience the attentive staff and serene elegance evocative of a gracious country estate. Conveniently situated near the theater, museums, golf and Tanglewood. Three hours from Boston or New York City. Albany Int'l. Airport: 50 miles/80 km, 45 minutes.

Worldwide Reservations
www.preferredhotels.com
+800 323 7500 USA/Canada
+00 800 3237 5001 Europe (UIFN)
Other areas: See page 204

BOSTON HARBOR HOTEL

ACCOMMODATIONS: 230 total guestrooms, including 26 suites, each room offering multi-line speakerphones, high-speed Internet access, Web TV, Nintendo, voice mail, mini-bar, newspaper, robes, slippers, umbrella and Molton Brown toiletries. VCR on request.

FACILITIES/SERVICES: Spa, fitness center, indoor pool, concierge, car rental, child care services, dry cleaning, shoe shine, florist, gift shop, valet parking and local town-car service. Pet-friendly accommodations, amenities and dog-walking services.

BUSINESS SERVICES: Business Center, Internet access, computer stations, secretarial and translating services.

DINING: At "Meritage-The Restaurant" experience the fusion of food and wine, boasting spectacular harbor views; "Intrigue Cafe" for casual indoor and seasonal outdoor dining; and "Rowes Wharf Bar" for cocktails and lighter fare.

MEETINGS: Total Meeting Rooms: 9 Total Sq. Ft.: 15,000 / Sq. M.: 1,396

RATES: USD 325.00 to 1,900.00; Corporate, Group, Package rates.

Mr. Paul Jacques, General Manager

Rowes Wharf
Boston, Massachusetts 02110, USA
Tel: +1 617 439 7000
Fax: +1 617 330 9450
Email: reservations@bhh.com
www.bhh.com

The waterfront hotel's 80-foot (24-meter) arch and golden-domed rotunda are complemented by handcarved wood, Italian marble and historic art. Yachts and sailboats glide on the harbor of this landmark hotel. Warm service welcomes guests to unforgettable comfort, style and elegance. "Boston's Best Hotel" by *Boston Magazine* for 2002 and rated as "One of the Top 100 Places to Stay" by *Condé Nast Traveler*. In the Financial District near museums, theaters and shopping. Logan Int'l. Airport: 1 mile/2 km, 10 minutes. Airport Water Shuttle: 0.5 miles/ 1 km, 7 minutes.

Worldwide Reservations
www.preferredhotels.com
+800 323 7500 USA/Canada
+00 800 3237 5001 Europe (UIFN)
Other areas: See page 204

THE CHARLES HOTEL, HARVARD SQUARE

Known as Boston's most original hotel, The Charles Hotel is simple, stylish and smart. Situated in the heart of Harvard Square, the intellectual center of the nation, The Charles Hotel offers modern décor in a historic yet energetic setting. Four blocks to the gates of Harvard Yard, and one block from the Charles River. Less than 10 minutes to Boston by car or subway. Logan Int'l. Airport: 7 miles/11 km, 15 minutes.

ACCOMMODATIONS: 293 total guestrooms, including 44 suites, each with Internet access, three multi-line phones, voice mail, mini-bar, robes, TV in all bathrooms, DVD player and Bose Wave radio. Views include the Boston skyline and Charles River.

FACILITIES/SERVICES: Tri-level fitness center with indoor pool, day spa, concierge, Avis car rental, dry cleaning and multilingual staff.

BUSINESS SERVICES: On-site Business Center, audio visual consultant and administrative services available.

DINING: Award-winning "Rialto" serves Mediterranean fusion cuisine. "Henrietta's Table" offers New England classics using fresh local ingredients. Live jazz at "Regattabar." "Noir" is perfect for cocktails.

MEETINGS: Total Meeting Rooms: 18 Total Sq. Ft.: 15,236 / Sq. M.: 1,418

RATES: USD 250.00 to 3,000.00; Corporate, Group, Package rates.

Mr. Alex Attia, General Manager

One Bennett Street/Harvard Square
Cambridge, Massachusetts 02138, USA
Tel: +1 617 864 1200
Fax: +1 617 864 5715
Email: generalmail@charleshotel.com
www.charleshotel.com

Worldwide Reservations
www.preferredhotels.com
+800 323 7500 USA/Canada
+00 800 3237 5001 Europe (UIFN)
Other areas: See page 204

CHOOSE THE PREFERRED WAY FOR BUSINESS TRAVEL WITH *PREFERRED BUSINESS PERKS*.

These days, trips are shorter but the stakes are much higher. With *Preferred Business Perks*, busy road warriors now can select the amenity of their choice. From January 1–December 31, 2004, participating hotels are offering your choice of one of the following *Preferred Business Perks*:

- Complimentary breakfast each day of your stay
- Complimentary parking each day of your stay
- Room upgrade based on availability

For more information and to book a *Preferred Business Perks* package, please visit our Web site at www.preferredhotels.com/offers, contact your travel professional or call 1 800 323 7500.

WEQUASSETT INN RESORT AND GOLF CLUB

ACCOMMODATIONS: 104 total guestrooms, including 6 suites, each with balcony or patio, data port, voice mail, coffee maker, newspaper and VCR on request.

FACILITIES/SERVICES: 18-hole golf course, pool, boating, croquet, volleyball, basketball, shuffleboard, horseshoes, fitness center, tennis, child care services, dry cleaning, concierge and shops.

BUSINESS SERVICES: Secretarial services available.

DINING: "Twenty-Eight Atlantic," a new elegant waterfront restaurant serving Progressive New England cuisine. "Thoreau's," a warm and intimate lounge. "The Outer Bar & Grille" offers an informal yet distinctive setting overlooking the bay.

MEETINGS: Total Meeting Rooms: 12 Total Sq. Ft.: 6,120 / Sq. M.: 570

RATES: USD 225.00 to 1,300.00; Group, Package rates.

Mr. Mark J. Novota,
Managing Partner

On Pleasant Bay
Chatham, Massachusetts 02633, USA
Tel: +1 508 432 5400
Fax: +1 508 432 5032
Email: fkiernan@wequassett.com
www.wequassett.com

This resort is nestled on 22 wooded acres with 20 buildings, including Cape Cod-style cottages and Colonial structures surrounded by carefully tended gardens. This secluded waterfront hideaway offers a relaxing atmosphere in a charming and intimate setting. On the seaward side of Cape Cod between Chatham and Orleans on Pleasant Bay. Hyannis Airport: 19 miles/31 km, 20 minutes. Boston Logan Int'l. Airport: 90 miles/145 km, 90 minutes.

Worldwide Reservations
www.preferredhotels.com
+800 323 7500 USA/Canada
+00 800 3237 5001 Europe (UIFN)
Other areas: See page 204

THE TOWNSEND HOTEL

Known as the locale of choice for metropolitan Detroit's affluent traveler, The Townsend is nestled among the tree-lined streets, shops and restaurants in this boutique suburban community. The beauty of the hotel lobby's Waterford chandeliers, flowers and marble fireplace is surpassed by the attention to detail of the award-winning hotel staff. The Townsend exudes charm and elegance. Located 20 minutes north of downtown. Detroit Metropolitan Airport: 25 miles/40 km, 40 minutes. Pontiac/Oakland County Airport: 20 miles/32 km, 30 minutes.

Worldwide Reservations

www.preferredhotels.com
+800 323 7500 USA/Canada
+00 800 3237 5001 Europe (UIFN)
Other areas: See page 204

ACCOMMODATIONS: 150 total guestrooms, including 55 suites, and 2 penthouse suites, all with interactive cable TV, Internet access, multi-line cordless phone with data port and voice mail, CD player, refreshment center and oversized safe. European bed linens, bathrobe and slippers, newspaper and coffee service for each room.

FACILITIES/SERVICES: Fitness center, concierge, walking distance to the area's finest restaurants, shopping and spas.

BUSINESS SERVICES: High-speed Internet connection, Business Center with Internet workstations, scanner, color printer and high-speed copier. Wireless high-speed Internet in all public guest areas.

DINING: The award-winning "Rugby Grille" offers breakfast, lunch and dinner daily. Evening nightspot—"The Corner"—open Wednesday through Saturday evening.

MEETINGS: Total Meeting Rooms: 7 Total Sq. Ft.: 9,300 / Sq. M.: 866

RATES: USD 275.00 to 1,500.00; Corporate, Group, Package rates.

Mr. Peter Wilde, Managing Director

100 Townsend Street
Birmingham, Michigan 48009, USA
Tel: +1 248 642 7900
Fax: +1 248 645 9061
Email: reservations@townsendhotel.com
www.townsendhotel.com

AMWAY GRAND PLAZA HOTEL

In the heart of Grand Rapids, the historic Amway Grand Plaza Hotel highlights English Adams architecture and North America's largest gold-leaf ceiling. The Amway Grand Plaza Hotel is where elegant old-world charm meets the spirit of the city. Located in the business district and connected to the convention center. Gerald R. Ford Int'l. Airport: 12 mi/ 19 km, 18 min.

ACCOMMODATIONS: 682 total guestrooms, including 49 suites, each with two multi-line phones, data port, voice mail, newspaper, hair dryer, robes and Internet.

FACILITIES/SERVICES: Concierge, shoe shine, fitness center, child care services, salon, tennis, dry cleaning, florist, shops, raquetball and indoor pool.

BUSINESS SERVICES: On-site Business Center and secretarial services available.

DINING: "The 1913 Room" features haute cuisine. "Cygnus Restaurant & Lounge" offers contemporary American cuisine, and the "GP Sports Bar & Restaurant" features grill items in a sports setting. "Bentham's Riverfront Restaurant" for all-day dining. "Cornucopia" deli for coffee, pastries and sandwiches.

MEETINGS: Total Meeting Rooms: 35 Total Sq. Ft.: 57,000 / Sq. M.: 5,307

RATES: USD 139.00 to 255.00; Corporate, Group, Package rates.

Mr. Richard Winn, General Manager

187 Monroe Avenue NW
Grand Rapids, Michigan 49503, USA
Tel: +1 616 774 2000
Fax: +1 616 776 6489
Email: reservations@amwaygrand.com
www.amwaygrand.com

Worldwide Reservations
www.preferredhotels.com
+800 323 7500 USA/Canada
+00 800 3237 5001 Europe (UIFN)
Other areas: See page 204

THE GRAND HOTEL MINNEAPOLIS

The Grand Hotel Minneapolis is the cities' highest rated and only luxury hotel. Casual elegance with world-class accommodations in a boutique-style atmosphere make this the Ultimate Urban Resort® in the heart of Minneapolis. Centrally located in the downtown business and financial district. Within walking distance and climate-controlled skyway access to theaters, shopping and entertainment. Minneapolis-St. Paul Int'l. Airport: 12 miles/20 km, 15 minutes.

ACCOMMODATIONS: 140 total guestrooms, including 17 suites, each featuring Tuscan-style décor with radio/CD players, high-speed Internet, two-line speaker phones, data port, voice mail, safes, mini-bar, turndown service with Godiva® chocolates, and large marble bathrooms, many with soaking tubs and TVs.

FACILITIES/SERVICES: 58,000-square-foot (5,400-square-meter) athletic facility with gymnasium, sauna, steam room, pool, aerobics and boxing studios, running track, basketball, squash, racquetball and handball courts. Aveda® concept Salon and Spa.

BUSINESS SERVICES: Business Center, private offices, boardrooms, video and teleconferencing and wireless Internet.

DINING: "Martini BLU", Twin Cities' hottest new restaurant and nightclub features award-winning sushi, martini creations and music. Intimate lobby bar boasts specialty cocktails and cigars. A Starbucks on property.

MEETINGS: Total Meeting Rooms: 7 Total Sq. Ft.: 8,000 / Sq. M.: 745

RATES: USD 259.00 to 3,500.00; Corporate, Group, Package rates.

Mr. Mark Peregory,
Vice President & Managing Director

Worldwide Reservations
www.preferredhotels.com
+800 323 7500 USA/Canada
+00 800 3237 5001 Europe (UIFN)
Other areas: See page 204

615 Second Avenue South
Minneapolis, Minnesota 55402, USA
Tel: +1 612 288 8888
Fax: +1 612 373 0407
Email: info@grandhotelminneapolis.com
www.grandhotelminneapolis.com

HOTEL PHILLIPS

Kansas City, Missouri, USA

ACCOMMODATIONS: 217 total guestrooms, including 2 suites, each with two multi-line phones, voice mail, high-speed Internet access in all guestrooms and meeting rooms, newspaper, bathrobes, iron & board, and coffee maker with complimentary coffee/tea. Fax machine on request.

FACILITIES/SERVICES: Fitness center, concierge, shoe shine and dry cleaning.

BUSINESS SERVICES: Business Center and secretarial services.

DINING: Adding to the guest experience are two diverse restaurants, each offering an outstanding dining experience. The "Phillips ChopHouse's" rich walnut and marble welcome you to one of Kansas City's premier steak houses. "12 Baltimore" is the perfect destination for lunch and dinner, and offers a near-perfect mix of top food and drink. It's downtown's place to see and be seen.

MEETINGS: Total Meeting Rooms: 8 Total Sq. Ft.: 5,763 / Sq. M.: 537

RATES: USD 129.00 to 219.00; Corporate, Group, Package rates.

Mr. Tom Pratt, General Manager

106 West 12th Street
Kansas City, Missouri 64105, USA
Tel: +1 816 221 7000
Fax: +1 816 221 3477
Email: tompratt@hotelphillips.com
www.hotelphillips.com

Hotel Phillips is a historical landmark that combines Art Deco ambiance with European-style luxury in the heart of downtown Kansas City. This contemporary yet inviting hotel creates an intimate refuge for today's business or leisure traveler. Hotel Phillips is ideally located two blocks from the Convention Center. Kansas City Int'l. Airport: 17 miles/28 km, 25 minutes. Downtown Executive Airport: .5 miles/ 1 km, 10 minutes.

Worldwide Reservations
www.preferredhotels.com
+800 323 7500 USA/Canada
+00 800 3237 5001 Europe (UIFN)
Other areas: See page 204

CHASE PARK PLAZA HOTEL

Following a recent $100 million renovation, the historic Chase Park Plaza Hotel features an array of indulgences. Located adjacent to Forest Park in the trendy Central West End, the hotel has exquisite décor and energetic ambiance. The vibrant neighborhood features fine grocers, salons, shops, restaurants, clubs and nightlife all within walking distance. The Chase Park Plaza is situated convenient to Downtown St. Louis (10 minutes), the Clayton business district (10 minutes), Metrolink rail system (5 minutes), and Lambert Int'l. Airport (20 minutes).

ACCOMMODATIONS: 251 total guestrooms, including 207 suites, each with two multi-line phones, data port, voice mail, newspaper, mini-bar, hair dryer, and high-speed wireless Internet service throughout the property.

FACILITIES/SERVICES: Spa, concierge, shoe shine, salon, dry cleaning, florist, shops, barber shop and tanning salon, five-screen movie theater and 18,000-square-foot health club.

BUSINESS SERVICES: On-site Business Center, secretarial services, audio visual services and wireless high-speed Internet.

DINING: Specializing in New American cuisine, the inviting "Eau Bistro" features fresh seafood and meats. With an emphasis on seasonal American cuisine, "Marquee Café" offers a range of delicious selections. "Tenderloin" restaurant is legendary for its masterfully seasoned steaks. "Chaser's" is a full-service bar adjacent to the hotel's theater.

MEETINGS: Total Meeting Rooms: 27 Total Sq. Ft.: 63,000 / Sq. M.: 5,853

RATES: USD 185.00 to 325.00 Corporate, Group, Package rates.

Mr. Bruce Westerlin, General Manager

Worldwide Reservations
www.preferredhotels.com
+800 323 7500 USA/Canada
+00 800 3237 5001 Europe (UIFN)
Other areas: See page 204

212-232 N. Kingshighway Blvd.
St. Louis, Missouri 63108, USA
Tel: +1 314 633 3000
Fax: +1 314 633 3003
Email: reservations@chaseparkplaza.com
www.chaseparkplaza.com

CLAYTON ON THE PARK, A HOTEL & RESIDENCE

ACCOMMODATIONS: 98 suites, each with a fully stocked kitchen, two multi-line phones, data port, voice mail, caller ID, newspaper, personal mini-bar shopping list, robes, hair dryer, magnified make-up mirror, full kitchen, coffee maker, toaster and VCRs available on request.

FACILITIES/SERVICES: Nutriformance Fitness Center, rooftop veranda with 360-degree views, concierge, child care services available and dry cleaning. Swimming, tennis and ice skating available across the street in Shaw Park, as well as extensive fitness facilities and two indoor pools.

BUSINESS SERVICES: Business Center and secretarial services, conference rooms, high-speed Internet wireless access and private offices.

DINING: Baseball Hall of Famer Ozzie Smith and Chef David Slay's "Smith & Slay's Restaurant and Bon Bar."

MEETINGS: Total Meeting Rooms: 6 Total Sq. Ft.: 10,833 / Sq. M.: 1,009

RATES: USD 185.00 to 325.00; Group, Package rates.

Mr. Micarl Hill, General Manager

8025 Bonhomme Avenue
Clayton/St. Louis, Missouri 63105, USA
Tel: +1 314 721 6543
Fax: +1 314 721 8588
Email: reservations@
claytononthepark.com
www.claytononthepark.com

This cosmopolitan hotel combines modern amenities with Midwestern hospitality. The contemporary lobby is accented with a giant saltwater aquarium housing a live coral reef, as well as an intimate sitting area with a warm glowing fireplace. Overlooking Shaw Park and its outdoor pools and tennis courts, Clayton on the Park is within walking distance to businesses, specialty stores, antique shops, art galleries and restaurants. Near the area's largest shopping center and attractions, Clayton is the business and social hub of the metropolitan St. Louis region. Lambert Int'l. Airport: 15 miles/24 km, 15 minutes.

Worldwide Reservations
www.preferredhotels.com
+800 323 7500   USA/Canada
+00 800 3237 5001   Europe (UIFN)
Other areas: See page 204

GREEN VALLEY RANCH RESORT & SPA

Only minutes from the world-famous Las Vegas Strip, the Green Valley Ranch Resort & Spa combines exciting casino action and nightlife with the relaxing ambiance of a luxury resort and spa. The resort's Mediterranean-style and unrivaled service make it the perfect place to stay for work, pleasure, business or relaxation. Situated minutes from four premier area golf courses: Dragon Ridge, Legacy, Revere and Rio Secco. McCarran Int'l. Airport: 5 miles/8 km, 5 minutes. Las Vegas Strip; 8 miles: complimentary scheduled shuttle service to both the Las Vegas Strip and McCarran Airport.

Worldwide Reservations
www.preferredhotels.com
+800 323 7500 USA/Canada
+00 800 3237 5001 Europe (UIFN)
Other areas: See page 204

ACCOMMODATIONS: 201 total guestrooms, including 45 suites, each with two phones, voice mail, data port, CD player, coffee maker, robes and down comforters.

FACILITIES/SERVICES: Overlooking the Las Vegas Strip, the resort features eight acres of gardens with spa and garden amphitheater surrounded by the hotel's vineyard. The pool features its own sandy beach and there is a casino, 35 retail establishments and eight restaurants adjacent to the resort. Fitness center, child care, concierge and salon available.

BUSINESS SERVICES: Business services available.

DINING: A variety of culinary fare at "Il Fornaio," "Gustav Mauler's-Bull Shrimp," "Fado's Irish Pub," "Sushi + Sake," "China Spice," "Trophy's Restaurant," "The Original Pancake House" and "The Feast Buffet."

MEETINGS: Total Meeting Rooms: 13 Total Sq. Ft.: 20,000 / Sq. M.: 1,862

RATES: USD 150.00 to 350.00; Corporate, Group, Package rates.

Mr. Joseph Hasson,
Vice President & General Manager

2300 Paseo Verde Parkway
Henderson, Nevada 89052, USA
Tel: +1 702 617 7777
Fax: +1 702 617 7778
Email: veronica.kistner@
stationcasinos.com
www.greenvalleyranchresort.com

INN OF THE ANASAZI

ACCOMMODATIONS: 59 total guestrooms, including 8 deluxe rooms, each with a gaslit fireplace, two phones, data port, voice mail, VCR, newspaper, safe, mini-bar, robes, coffee, and iron & board.

FACILITIES/SERVICES: Room service, concierge, child care services, dry cleaning and shoe shine. New exercise facility available July 15, 2004.

BUSINESS SERVICES: The front desk can take care of most business needs. Computers, Internet access, etc., are available for rental.

DINING: The "Anasazi Restaurant" features award-winning contemporary Southwestern cuisine for breakfast, lunch and dinner.

MEETINGS: Total Meeting Rooms: 3 Total Sq. Ft.: 1,100 / Sq. M.: 77

RATES: USD 199.00 to 475.00; Mr. Jeff Mahan, General Manager

113 Washington Avenue
Santa Fe, New Mexico 87501, USA
Tel: +1 505 988 3030
Fax: +1 505 988 3277
Email: reservations@
innoftheanasazi.com
www.innoftheanasazi.com

An intimate and romantic world-class inn and restaurant featuring traditional Pueblo-style architecture, authentic artwork and four-poster beds. Nestled in the heart of Santa Fe's historic district, the Inn is a haven for travelers. Located just steps from Santa Fe's Plaza at the base of the Sangre de Cristo Mountains. Golf, horseback riding, spa, Anasazi ruins, museums and other outdoor activities are nearby. Albuquerque Int'l. Airport: 60 miles/97 km, 60 minutes.

Worldwide Reservations
www.preferredhotels.com
+800 323 7500 USA/Canada
+00 800 3237 5001 Europe (UIFN)
Other areas: See page 204

85

THE SAGAMORE

Situated in the unspoiled Adirondack Mountains, The Sagamore is a private island resort on Lake George in upstate New York. Guests enjoy comfortable accommodations in the Historic Hotel and the Adirondack-style Lodges and a choice of dining at six extraordinary restaurants. The Sagamore, which features a Donald Ross championship golf course and European-style spa, is a year-round sports paradise. At Bolton Landing, on its own 72-acre island. Albany Int'l. Airport: 65 miles/105 km, 75 minutes.

ACCOMMODATIONS: 350 total guestrooms, including 176 suites, with lake view and garden view rooms. The Adirondack-style Lodges feature rooms and suites and terraces.

FACILITIES/SERVICES: Golf, tennis courts, spa, pool, private beach, sailing, fitness center, boating, children's programs and shops. Cross-country skiing, sledding and ice skating. Downhill skiing nearby.

BUSINESS SERVICES: Recently enhanced Business Center available.

DINING: "Trillium" for American Contemporary cuisine; the "Sagamore Dining Room" for regional and international selections; "Club Grill;" "Mister Brown's Pub" for casual dining; "The Morgan," a 19th-century touring vessel; "The Veranda" for afternoon tea, cocktails, tapas and sushi; and "The Pavillion" for lakeside seasonal lobster bakes.

MEETINGS: Total Meeting Rooms: 19 Total Sq. Ft.: 26,000 / Sq. M.: 2,421

RATES: USD 149.00 to 709.00; Corporate, Group, Package rates.

Mr. S. Lee Bowden, Managing Director

110 Sagamore Road, P.O. Box 450 Bolton Landing, New York 12814, USA Tel: +1 518 644 9400 Fax: +1 518 743 6036 Email: reserve@thesagamore.com www.thesagamore.com

Worldwide Reservations
www.preferredhotels.com
+800 323 7500 USA/Canada
+00 800 3237 5001 Europe (UIFN)
Other areas: See page 204

THE ST. REGIS NEW YORK

A 1904 Beaux Arts landmark, The St. Regis New York reigns as the flagship of The St. Regis brand. Situated along Fifth Avenue, this hotel offers a Midtown oasis with Louis XVI decorated guestrooms, silk wall coverings and spacious marble baths. Located near Central Park, Rockefeller Center, museums and theaters. Within walking distance to shopping on Fifth Avenue and Madison Avenue. John F. Kennedy Int'l. Airport: 17 miles/ 27 km. LaGuardia Airport: 10 miles/16 km. Newark Int'l. Airport: 18 miles/29km.

ACCOMMODATIONS: 222 total guestrooms, including 93 suites, each with 24-hour butler service, multi-line phone, high-speed Internet access, voice mail, fax, VCR, CD player, mini-bar, robes and hair dryer. Welcome amenity, pressing of two garments per guest, tea or coffee upon arrival and with wake-up call, complimentary shoe shine, newspaper and mineral water at turndown.

FACILITIES/SERVICES: Fitness center, spa, dry cleaning, hair salon, and on-site florist.

BUSINESS SERVICES: Business Center, high-speed Internet access, color printer, secretarial and translating services available.

DINING: Afternoon tea or American cuisine in "Astor Court." Visit our "King Cole Bar & Lounge," where the "Red Snapper" (now the Bloody Mary) was invented and Maxfield Parish's famous mural presides.

MEETINGS: Total Meeting Rooms: 13 Total Sq. Ft.: 16,385 / Sq. M.: 1,525

RATES: USD 600.00 to 11,500.00; Corporate, Group, Package rates.

Mr. Guenter Richter, Managing Director

  @

---

2 East 55th Street
New York, New York 10022, USA
Tel: +1 212 753 4500
Fax: +1 212 787 3447
Email: stregisny.res@stregis.com
www.stregis.com

Worldwide Reservations
www.preferredhotels.com
+800 323 7500 USA/Canada
+00 800 3237 5001 Europe (UIFN)
Other areas: See page 204

THE GARDEN CITY HOTEL

ACCOMMODATIONS: 280 total guestrooms, including 16 suites, each with two phones, data port, voice mail, newspaper, safe, mini-bar and robes. VCR on request.

FACILITIES/SERVICES: Fitness center, indoor swimming pool, Jacuzzi, sauna, wireless Internet, dry cleaning, shoe shine, salon and gift shop.

BUSINESS SERVICES: Business Center, secretarial and translating services, and notary public available. Courier service, fax services, office supplies.

DINING: "The Polo Restaurant" offers New American cuisine by Executive Chef Steven DeBruyn. The *New York Times* describes the atmosphere as "opulent and sophisticated" and the service as "attentive, amiable and well informed." "The Rein Bar & Grill," just off the lobby, features an inviting fireplace, plasma TV screens and music nightly.

MEETINGS: Total Meeting Rooms: 16 Total Sq. Ft.: 25,000 / Sq. M.: 2,328

RATES: USD 275.00 to 2,150.00; Corporate, Group, Package rates.

Mr. Nasser Samman,
General Manager

45 Seventh Street
Garden City, New York 11530, USA
Tel: +1 516 747 3000
Fax: +1 516 747 1414
Email: info@gchotel.com
www.gardencityhotel.com

On the site where its famed predecessor was built in 1874, The Garden City Hotel offers the charm of the Old World combined with the conveniences of today. From its scenic village locale just outside New York City, guests experience the grandeur of the metropolitan area without the distractions of urban life. Garden City, on New York's Long Island, is a quaint village that boasts tree-lined streets, boutiques, trendy nightspots, restaurants and cafes. JFK Int'l. Airport: 12 miles/19 km, 16 minutes. La Guardia Airport: 16 miles/26 km, 22 minutes.

Worldwide Reservations
www.preferredhotels.com
+800 323 7500 USA/Canada
+00 800 3237 5001 Europe (UIFN)
Other areas: See page 204

BALLANTYNE RESORT

Ballantyne Resort signals the return of the "Grand Hotel." Nestled in the gently rolling hills of North Carolina, Ballantyne Resort welcomes guests to a world of elegant architecture, gracious service and uncompromising quality in a true resort setting. Prominently set in Ballantyne, Charlotte's premier neighborhood, the resort is within walking distance of shops and restaurants. Charlotte/Douglas Int'l. Airport: 12 miles/20 km, 20 minutes.

ACCOMMODATIONS: 214 total guestrooms, including 15 suites, each with two multi-line phones, voice mail, data port, robes, hair dryer, iron & board, newspaper, safe and high-speed Internet access. VCR available on request.

FACILITIES/SERVICES: 18-hole, par-71 golf course, tennis courts, spa, concierge, shoe shine, fitness center, salon, tennis, dry cleaning and shops.

BUSINESS SERVICES: On-site Business Center and secretarial services available.

DINING: With sweeping views of the 18th fairway, "The Grill Room" offers extravagant daily breakfasts and luncheon buffets. For dinner, the warm and intimate "Club Room" offers à la carte specialties with an international flair.

MEETINGS: Total Meeting Rooms: 23 Total Sq. Ft.: 25,000 / Sq. M.: 1,490

RATES: USD 229.00 to 1,200.00; Corporate, Group, Package rates.

Mr. Wayne C. Shusko, Managing Director

10000 Ballantyne Commons Parkway
Charlotte, North Carolina 28277, USA
Tel: +1 704 248 4000
Fax: +1 704 248 4005
Email: info@ballantyneresort.com
www.ballantyneresort.com

Worldwide Reservations
www.preferredhotels.com
+800 323 7500 USA/Canada
+00 800 3237 5001 Europe (UIFN)
Other areas: See page 204

THE PARK HOTEL

ACCOMMODATIONS: 192 total guestrooms, including 8 suites, each with two phones, data port, voice mail, safe, high-speed Internet access and robes. VCR available on request.

FACILITIES/SERVICES: Health club, concierge, shoe shine and nearby golf at Ballantyne Golf Club.

BUSINESS SERVICES: On-site Business Center.

DINING: Enjoy a diverse menu at "Smoky's Grill" in a relaxed and comfortable atmosphere, or cocktails in the adjoining bar, richly appointed in mahogany and leather.

MEETINGS: Total Meeting Rooms: 10 Total Sq. Ft.: 8,102 / Sq. M.: 754

RATES: USD 139.00 to 1,200.00; Group, Package rates.

Mr. Michael Zubel, General Manager

2200 Rexford Road
Charlotte, North Carolina 28211, USA
Tel: +1 704 364 8220
Fax: +1 704 365 4712
Email: reserve@theparkhotel.com
www.theparkhotel.com

Traditional architecture, period furnishings and a large art collection make The Park Hotel a cozy retreat or a comfortable headquarters for business. Nestled in the South Park neighborhood, the hotel is surrounded by upscale shops, restaurants and boutiques. The hotel features a warm and friendly staff as well as intimate and elegant furnishings. Located within 20 minutes of the theater district, performing arts venues and uptown business district. Charlotte/Douglas Int'l. Airport: 10 miles/16 km, 20 minutes.

Worldwide Reservations
www.preferredhotels.com
+800 323 7500   USA/Canada
+00 800 3237 5001   Europe (UIFN)
Other areas: See page 204

THE CINCINNATIAN HOTEL

Built in 1882, The Cincinnatian Hotel features European décor, traditional architecture and a large art collection. Nestled downtown, the hotel is in the heart of upscale shops and restaurants. Unforgettable accommodations, memorable dining and stellar service all make this hotel a cozy retreat or comfortable business headquarters. Located one block from Fountain Square, near the Aronoff Center for the Arts, Contemporary Art Center, Convention Center, sports stadiums. Greater Cincinnati/ N. Kentucky Int'l. Airport: 13 miles/21 km, 20 minutes.

ACCOMMODATIONS: 146 total guestrooms, including 8 suites, each with two multi-line phones, data port, complimentary high-speed Internet access, voice mail in four languages, newspaper, safe, mini-bar, hair dryer and robes. VCR on request.

FACILITIES/SERVICES: Garden bath, whirlpool, or electric fireplace available, fitness center, concierge, child care services, dry cleaning, shoe shine and florist.

BUSINESS SERVICES: Secretarial services available.

DINING: Dine on French-American cuisine in the elegant "Palace Restaurant," then relax in "The Cricket Lounge" with a nightcap.

MEETINGS: Total Meeting Rooms: 6 Total Sq. Ft.: 3,157 / Sq. M.: 294

RATES: USD 225.00 to 1,500.00; Corporate, Group, Package rates.

Mrs. Denise Vandersall, Managing Director

601 Vine Street
Cincinnati, Ohio 45202, USA
Tel: +1 513 381 3000
Fax: +1 513 651 0256
Email: info@cincinnatianhotel.com
www.cincinnatianhotel.com

Worldwide Reservations
www.preferredhotels.com
+800 323 7500 USA/Canada
+00 800 3237 5001 Europe (UIFN)
Other areas: See page 204

ACCOMMODATIONS: 150 total guestrooms, including 33 suites, each with two multi-line phones, data port, high-speed Internet access, voice mail, newspaper, French-press coffee, CD alarm clock radio, hair dryer, mini-bar, robes and access to a 400-title complimentary movie library.

FACILITIES/SERVICES: Fitness center, concierge, tea service, slippers with turndown and dry cleaning.

BUSINESS SERVICES: Secretarial, translating services and work station with color printer, scanner and fax.

DINING: The James Beard Award-winning "Heathman Restaurant" features French cuisine with Pacific Northwest ingredients.

MEETINGS: Total Meeting Rooms: 8 Total Sq. Ft.: 3,495 / Sq. M.: 325

RATES: USD 150.00 to 750.00; Corporate, Group, Package rates.

Mr. Jeff Jobe, General Manager

1001 S.W. Broadway
Portland, Oregon 97205, USA
Tel: +1 503 241 4100
Fax: +1 503 790 7110
Email: info@heathmanhotel.com
www.heathmanhotel.com

Built in 1927, The Heathman is an artistic masterpiece, a timeless classic offering attentive service by a "Personal Concierge." Recognized as one of the "Top 100 Hotels" in the U.S. and Canada in 2002 by *Travel & Leisure* magazine. Guests can lose themselves in the original art throughout the hotel or revel in the sounds of jazz in the signature "Tea Court." In the heart of downtown Portland's Cultural District and next to the Portland Center for Performing Arts. Portland Int'l. Airport: 9 miles/15 km, 20 minutes.

Worldwide Reservations
www.preferredhotels.com
+800 323 7500 USA/Canada
+00 800 3237 5001 Europe (UIFN)
Other areas: See page 204

THE HOTEL HERSHEY®

THE HOTEL HERSHEY offers a mix of European splendor set amid the picturesque countryside and is reminiscent of the dreams of its founder, Chocolate King Milton S. Hershey. Styled after a 19th-century Mediterranean resort, the hotel offers state-of-the-art amenities, including The Spa At THE HOTEL HERSHEY® and championship golf at HERSHEY® Golf Club, along with the charm of restored balustrades, original mosaic tiles and hand-sculpted fountains. Close to Pennsylvania Dutch Country, Gettysburg and HERSHEYPARK®. Harrisburg Int'l. Airport: 15 miles/24 km, 20 minutes.

ACCOMMODATIONS: 232 total guestrooms, including 25 suites, each with three multi-line phones, data port, voice mail, CD player, newspaper, hair dryers and robes.

FACILITIES/SERVICES: Spa, fitness center, tennis, indoor/outdoor pools, bocce court, basketball and volleyball courts, carriage rides, jogging/walking/mountain-bike trails, championship golf, concierge, and limousine.

BUSINESS SERVICES: Business Center, high-speed Internet access and secretarial service.

DINING: Contemporary American cuisine in the award-winning "Circular Dining Room," casual dining in "The Fountain Cafe," seasonal fare at the "Club House Cafe & Creamery," or cocktails and light fare at the "Iberian Lounge." Cappuccino and pastries in the "Cocoa Beanery."

MEETINGS: Total Meeting Rooms: 20 Total Sq. Ft.: 22,000 / Sq. M.: 2,048

RATES: USD 219.00 to 2,500.00; Corporate, Group, Package rates.

Mr. Brian R. O'Day, General Manager

Hotel Road
Hershey, Pennsylvania 17033, USA
Tel: +1 717 533 2171
Fax: +1 717 534 8887
Email: info@hersheypa.com
www.thehotelhershey.com

Worldwide Reservations
www.preferredhotels.com
+800 323 7500 USA/Canada
+00 800 3237 5001 Europe (UIFN)
Other areas: See page 204

THE SANCTUARY AT KIAWAH ISLAND

Charleston, South Carolina, USA

ACCOMMODATIONS: 255 total guestrooms, including 13 suites, each with three dual-line phones, data port, voice mail, VCR on request, newspaper, CD/DVD player, safe, mini-bar, robes and hair dryer. Complimentary high-speed and wireless Internet access available.

FACILITIES/SERVICES: Club level, five championship golf courses, concierge, spa, shoe shine, fitness center, child care services, salon, tennis, dry cleaning, florist and shops. Hiking, kayaking and canoeing, and beach services also available.

BUSINESS SERVICES: Business Center with secretarial and translating services and private meeting rooms.

DINING: Two ocean-view restaurants, including "The Ocean Room," which features the freshest available seafood and local produce. There are also two bars and an oceanfront pool bar.

MEETINGS: Total Meeting Rooms: 8 Total Sq. Ft.: 18,000 / Sq. M.: 1,676

RATES: USD 275.00 to 4,500.00; Corporate, Group, Package rates.

Mr. Prem Devadas,
Managing Director

12 Kiawah Beach Drive
Kiawah Island, South Carolina 29455,
USA
Tel: +1 843 768 6000
Fax: +1 843 768 6099
Email: sanctuary@kiawahresort.com
www.kiawahresort.com

Located on a 10-mile-long barrier island noted for its beauty and championship golf, The Sanctuary at Kiawah Island will become known as America's next great seaside resort. The Sanctuary has been carefully woven into the island's landscape using rarely used materials like copper, slate and hand-molded brick. Guests not only step into a grand seaside resort, they are brought into an exceptional ambiance suffused with Southern warmth. Opening March 2004. Located just 21 miles/34 km from historic Charleston and the city's famed cultural and dining attractions. Charleston Int'l Airport: 30 miles/45 km, 45 minutes.

Worldwide Reservations
www.preferredhotels.com
+800 323 7500 USA/Canada
+00 800 3237 5001 Europe (UIFN)
Other areas: See page 204

ACCOMMODATIONS: 464 total guestrooms, including 15 suites, each with multi-line phones, data port, voice mail and newspaper. VCR on request.

FACILITIES/SERVICES: Pool, fitness center, massage, sauna, steam room, whirlpool, aerobics, dry cleaning, shoe shine, salon and shops.

BUSINESS SERVICES: Business Center available.

DINING: Choose "Chez Philippe," the only Four Star-rated restaurant in the mid-South region, for classic French cuisine and "Capriccio Grill," featuring prime steak, seafood and pasta.

MEETINGS: Total Meeting Rooms: 36 Total Sq. Ft.: 80,000 / Sq. M.: 7,448

RATES: USD 199.00 to 1,675.00; Corporate, Group, Package rates.

Mr. Doug Browne, General Manager

149 Union Avenue
Memphis, Tennessee 38103, USA
Tel: +1 901 529 4000
Fax: +1 901 529 3600
Email: pmreservations@
peabodymemphis.com
www.peabodymemphis.com

Known as the South's Grand Hotel and built in 1925 in Italian Renaissance style, The Peabody features a magnificent Grand Lobby, high tea and the famous Peabody Marching Ducks. In the downtown Memphis business district, adjacent to the Peabody Place Entertainment & Retail Complex Center. Walking distance to Memphis Cook Convention Center, two blocks to Beale Street, "Home of the Blues," and a short drive to Graceland, The National Civil Rights Museum and other attractions. Memphis Int'l. Airport: 12 miles/19 km, 15 minutes.

Worldwide Reservations
www.preferredhotels.com
+800 323 7500 USA/Canada
+00 800 3237 5001 Europe (UIFN)
Other areas: See page 204

THE HERMITAGE HOTEL

Recently renovated, this luxurious historic hotel is one of Nashville's only remaining commercial Beaux Arts structures. Centrally located downtown, adjacent to the State Capitol Building and within walking distance of all major business and entertainment venues, The Hermitage Hotel offers a warm and elegant sanctuary within the city, as well as the finest accommodations and service in all of Nashville. Nashville Int'l. Airport: 10 miles/16 km, 15 minutes.

ACCOMMODATIONS: 123 total guestrooms, including 4 suites, each luxurious and oversized room features down-filled duvets, designer soaps, marble bathrooms, three multi-line phones, data port, newspaper, CD/DVD player, safe, mini-bar, robes and hair dryer.

FACILITIES/SERVICES: Concierge, shoe shine, laundry/dry cleaning service, sundries shop. Fitness center features strength equipment, as well as TVs on elliptical machines, bikes and treadmills. Massage therapy rooms with lockers and showers.

BUSINESS SERVICES: Business Services, secretarial and translating services.

DINING: The renowned "Capitol Grille Restaurant" serves all meals and features evening entertainment and Nashville's best Sunday Brunch. "The Oak Bar" has been meticulously restored and is a favorite retreat.

MEETINGS: Total Meeting Rooms: 5 Total Sq. Ft.: 5,271 / Sq. M.: 491

RATES: USD 195.00 to 1,500.00; Corporate, Group, Package rates.

Mr. Greg Sligh, General Manager

231 Sixth Avenue North
Nashville, Tennessee 37219, USA
Tel: +1 615 244 3121
Fax: +1 615 254 6909
Email: reservations@
thehermitagehotel.com
www.thehermitagehotel.com

Worldwide Reservations
www.preferredhotels.com
+800 323 7500   USA/Canada
+00 800 3237 5001   Europe (UIFN)
Other areas: See page 204

HOTEL DEREK

ACCOMMODATIONS: 314 total guestrooms, including 10 suites, each with two dual-line cordless phones, voice mail, data port, Internet access, CD clock radio, VCR on request, newspaper, safe, mini-bar. Fax machine available in some rooms and Internet access via TV.

FACILITIES/SERVICES: Concierge, child care services, shoe shine, complimentary three-mile radius local transportation, dry cleaning, evening turndown service and valet parking for all guests. 24-hour fitness center with spa treatment suite.

BUSINESS SERVICES: Business Center, secretarial services and 16 studio rooms with business alcoves offering fax/copier/printer, television.

DINING: "Maverick" restaurant serves regional and Southwestern cuisine in a warm, gallery-like setting. The bar and lobby lounge have intimate alcoves for cocktails.

MEETINGS: Total Meeting Rooms: 9 Total Sq. Ft.: 10,250 / Sq. M.: 954

RATES: USD 245.00 to 875.00; Corporate, Group, Package rates.

Mr. Steven Andre, General Manager

2525 West Loop South
Houston, Texas 77027, USA
Tel: +1 713 961 3000
Fax: +1 713 297 4392
Email: derek@hotelderek.com
www.hotelderek.com

With its crisp, tailored look, custom-designed furnishings, original artwork and contemporary pieces, Hotel Derek creates a bold international style, simultaneously celebrating its Texas heritage. Hotel Derek reflects all the energy and sophistication the city has to offer. Located in Uptown Houston, opposite the Galleria and convenient to downtown, Reliant Park, George R. Brown Convention Center, Minute Maid Park, Toyota Arena and the Texas Medical Center. Bush Intercontinental Airport: 25 miles/41 km, 35 minutes. Hobby Airport: 15 miles/24 km, 25 minutes.

Worldwide Reservations
www.preferredhotels.com
+800 323 7500 USA/Canada
+00 800 3237 5001 Europe (UIFN)
Other areas: See page 204

HOTEL ICON

Hotel ICON...a Personal Luxury Hotel...
is an experience in opulence while enlivening
the senses. With its historic façade and
classic-contemporary décor, furnishings and
artwork, this 1911 bank building provides
individual services and accommodations.
Near Houston's arts and entertainment
district, Hotel ICON is in the heart of the
business center and is within walking
distance to the George R. Brown Convention
Center, the Toyota Center, Minute Maid
Ballpark and the theater district. Bush Int'l.
Airport: 25 miles/40 km, 40 minutes. Hobby
Airport: 15 miles/24 km, 25 minutes.

Worldwide Reservations

www.preferredhotels.com
+800 323 7500 USA/Canada
+00 800 3237 5001 Europe (UIFN)
Other areas: See page 204

ACCOMMODATIONS: 135 total
guestrooms, including 9 signature
suites, each with two multi-line
phones, high-speed Internet access,
data port and voice mail, CD player,
safe, mini-bar, robes and hair dryer.

FACILITIES/SERVICES: Fitness
center, day spa, concierge, shoe
shine and child care services.
On-site transportation also available.

BUSINESS SERVICES: Business
Center, secretarial and translating
services and a videoconferencing
boardroom.

DINING: World-renowned chef
Jean-Georges Vongerichten's
restaurant, BANK, treats guests to an
unforgettable culinary experience.
The chic "Whiskey Bar," created by
nightlife impresario Rande Gerber, is
a stylish den of luxury where guests
relax as if in their own living room.

MEETINGS: Total Meeting Rooms: 5
Total Sq. Ft.: 5,000 / Sq. M.: 466

RATES: USD 245.00 to 2,500.00;
Corporate, Group, Package rates.

Mr. Troy Bennett, Managing Director

220 Main
Houston, Texas 77002, USA
Tel: +1 713 224 4266
Fax: +1 713 223 3223
Email: rreed@
benchmarkmanagement.com
www.hotelicon.com

THE HOUSTONIAN HOTEL, CLUB & SPA

ACCOMMODATIONS: 288 total guestrooms, including 8 suites, each with two multi-line cordless phones, data port, voice mail, mini-bar and safe. VCR on request.

FACILITIES/SERVICES: Nationally recognized Houstonian Club offers 100 group exercise classes each week, 200 exercise machines, tennis, paddleball, racquetball, squash courts, rock climbing wall, running tracks, pools and a children's gymnasium. Concierge, child care services and shops also available. New spa offers the most current treatments available.

BUSINESS SERVICES: Business Center, secretarial service, computers with Internet access and wireless Internet service.

DINING: "Olivette" combines ancient culinary traditions of the Mediterranean with American touches. "The Manor House" features superb cuisine, gorgeous views and a refined atmosphere.

MEETINGS: Total Meeting Rooms: 26 Total Sq. Ft.: 33,000 / Sq. M.: 3,072

RATES: USD 295.00 to 1,800.00; Corporate, Group, Package rates.

Mr. Mark S. Yanke,
Vice President & Managing Director

111 North Post Oak Lane
Houston, Texas 77024, USA
Tel: +1 713 680 2626
Fax: +1 713 680 2992
Email: sales2004@houstonian.com
www.houstonian.com

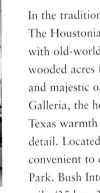

In the tradition of a grand Texas lodge, The Houstonian blends modern comforts with old-world charm. Nestled on 18 wooded acres (7 hectares) of towering pines and majestic oaks in the heart of the Galleria, the hotel extends expressions of Texas warmth and hospitality to every detail. Located in uptown Houston and convenient to downtown and Memorial Park. Bush Intercontinental Airport: 22 miles/35 km, 30 minutes.

Worldwide Reservations
www.preferredhotels.com
+800 323 7500   USA/Canada
+00 800 3237 5001   Europe (UIFN)
Other areas: See page 204

LA MANSIÓN DEL RIO

Situated along the romantic San Antonio River Walk, this Spanish Colonial mansion is an intimate hotel where old-world charm mingles with the excitement and energy of an international city. Downtown on the San Antonio River Walk, within easy walking distance of the Alamo, the convention center and other attractions. San Antonio Int'l. Airport: 12 miles/19 km, 20 minutes.

ACCOMMODATIONS: 337 total guestrooms, including 11 suites, each with three multi-line phones, data port, high-speed broadband Internet access, voice mail, mini-bar, robes, Web TV, hair dryers, iron & board, and coffee maker. VCR on request.

FACILITIES/SERVICES: Heated pool, fitness center, concierge, child care services, spa, dry cleaning, shoe shine.

BUSINESS SERVICES: On-site Business Center and secretarial services available.

DINING: "Las Canarias" is an award-winning culinary destination located on the romantic River Walk. Enjoy New American cuisine with regional influences prepared by nationally recognized Chef Scott Cohen.

MEETINGS: Total Meeting Rooms: 14 Total Sq. Ft.: 15,000 / Sq. M.: 1,396

RATES: USD 199.00 to 1,900.00; Corporate, Group, Package rates.

Mr. Michael Bazar, General Manager

112 College Street
San Antonio, Texas 78205, USA
Tel: +1 210 518 1000
Fax: +1 210 226 0389
Email: lmdr@lamansion.com
www.lamansion.com

Worldwide Reservations
www.preferredhotels.com
+800 323 7500 USA/Canada
+00 800 3237 5001 Europe (UIFN)
Other areas: See page 204

ACCOMMODATIONS: 99 total guestrooms, including 2 suites, each with three phones (two with multiple lines), data port, high-speed Internet access, voice mail, VCR on request, newspaper, fax, CD player, safe, robes, separate shower and Jacuzzi tub.

FACILITIES/SERVICES: Concierge, child care, salon, dry cleaning, shops, a 17,000-square-foot spa & fitness center, and an outdoor pool and hot tub.

BUSINESS SERVICES: Secretarial and translating services.

DINING: "Pesca on the River" has innovative recipes from acclaimed Chef Jonathan Parker featuring fresh fish delivered daily. The centerpiece of the restaurant is a high-octane, fiber optic-lit oyster bar offering signature cocktails, crafted beers, and wines by the glass.

MEETINGS: Total Meeting Rooms: 3 Total Sq. Ft.: 2,600 / Sq. M.: 242

RATES: USD 269.00 to 750.00; Corporate, Group, Package rates.

Mr. Michael Bazar, General Manager

212 West Crockett Street
San Antonio, Texas 78205, USA
Tel: +1 210 396 5800
Fax: +1 210 226 0389
Email: reservations@watermarkhotel.com
www.watermarkhotel.com

Within Watermark's inviting interior, warm woods, natural stone, hand-forged iron and expansive windows embrace guests in the comfortable elegance of a private residence. This intimate hotel, nestled along San Antonio's legendary River Walk, is the ideal place to combine business with pleasure, host a memorable event or relax in a serene sanctuary. Downtown on the San Antonio River Walk, within easy walking distance of the Alamo, the convention center and other attractions. San Antonio Int'l. Airport: 12 miles/19 km, 20 minutes.

Worldwide Reservations
www.preferredhotels.com
+800 323 7500 USA/Canada
+00 800 3237 5001 Europe (UIFN)
Other areas: See page 204

STEIN ERIKSEN LODGE

This European-style lodge exudes rustic Norwegian elegance and old-world charm with its beamed cathedral ceilings and great stone fireplaces. Nestled amid aspens and pines, high in the Rocky Mountains, the lodge is a blend of Alpine splendor with refined accommodations and attentive service. Located in Silver Lake Village, mid-mountain at Deer Valley Resort. Salt Lake City Int'l. Airport: 38 miles/61 km, 45 minutes.

ACCOMMODATIONS: 170 total guestrooms, including 58 suites, each with multi-line phones, data port, voice mail, Internet access, CD player, VCR/DVD, safe, mini-bar, robes, hair dryer and bottled water.

FACILITIES/SERVICES: Snow skiing, pool, spa, snowmobiling, cross-country skiing, mountain biking, hiking, golf, tennis, hot air ballooning, fitness center, shopping, fine dining, child care services and concierge.

BUSINESS SERVICES: Business Center and secretarial services.

DINING: "The Glitretind Restaurant" features an extensive wine list and gourmet cuisine in a warm, elegant setting.

MEETINGS: Total Meeting Rooms: 10 Total Sq. Ft.: 5,800 / Sq. M.: 540

RATES: USD 205.00 to 3,000.00; Group, Package rates.

Mr. Russ Olsen, Vice President & Managing Director

7700 Stein Way, P.O. Box 3177
Park City, Utah 84060, USA
Tel: +1 435 649 3700
Fax: +1 435 649 5825
Email: info@steinlodge.com
www.steinlodge.com

Worldwide Reservations
www.preferredhotels.com
+800 323 7500 USA/Canada
+00 800 3237 5001 Europe (UIFN)
Other areas: See page 204

TOPNOTCH AT STOWE RESORT & SPA

Natural woods and earth tones complement the contemporary design of this resort, which is nestled at the foot of Vermont's highest peak, Mount Mansfield, on 120 spectacular acres (49 hectares) of New England countryside. Topnotch at Stowe Resort & Spa offers the perfect balance of scenery, unrivaled accommodations, amenities and some of the most exquisite cuisine in the Northeast. In the Green Mountains, 4 miles/6 km from the historic village of Stowe and 1.5 miles/ 2 km from the ski slopes. Burlington Int'l. Airport: 35 miles/56 km, 40 minutes.

Worldwide Reservations
www.preferredhotels.com
+800 323 7500 USA/Canada
+00 800 3237 5001 Europe (UIFN)
Other areas: See page 204

ACCOMMODATIONS: 90 total guestrooms, including 13 suites, and 22 townhomes, each with voice mail, data port, in-room movies, newspaper, mini-refrigerator, robes, iron & board, safe, hair dryer and coffee maker.

FACILITIES/SERVICES: Tennis courts, pools, fitness center, whirlpool, sauna, equestrian center, biking trails, cross-country and downhill skiing, spa and salon.

BUSINESS SERVICES: Business Center and secretarial services.

DINING: Topnotch's award-winning chef creates gourmet cuisine in the main dining room, "Maxwell's at Topnotch." "The Buttertub Bistro and Lounge" offers nightly entertainment and light fare.

MEETINGS: Total Meeting Rooms: 6 Total Sq. Ft.: 10,000 / Sq. M.: 931

RATES: USD 250.00 to 750.00; Corporate, Group, Package rates.

Mr. Reggie Cooper,
President & General Manager

4000 Mountain Road
Stowe, Vermont 05672, USA
Tel: +1 802 253 8585
Fax: +1 802 253 9263
Email: info@topnotchresort.com
www.topnotch-resort.com

THE JEFFERSON HOTEL

ACCOMMODATIONS: 264 total guestrooms, including 36 suites, each with three multi-line phones, data port, voice mail, complimentary newspaper, CD player, safe, mini-bar, hair dryer and robes. VCR available on request.

FACILITIES/SERVICES: Indoor pool, fitness center with free weights, concierge, complimentary wireless Internet access, babysitting, dry cleaning, complimentary downtown transportation, salon, florist and shops.

BUSINESS SERVICES: On-site Business Center, secretarial and translating services available.

DINING: "Lemaire" featuring upscale Southern regional seasonal cuisine and "TJ's Restaurant and Lounge" for less formal dining.

MEETINGS: Total Meeting Rooms: 18 Total Sq. Ft.: 26,000 / Sq. M.: 2,421

RATES: USD 285.00 to 1,800.00; Corporate, Group, Package rates.

Mr. Joseph Longo, General Manager

101 West Franklin Street
Richmond, Virginia 23220, USA
Tel: +1 804 788 8000
Fax: +1 804 225 0334
Email: jefferson.sales@
jeffersonhotel.com
www.jeffersonhotel.com

Nestled in the heart of Richmond's charming downtown historic district and built in 1895, this Beaux Arts hotel is renowned for its breathtaking public spaces, luxurious accommodations and unsurpassed genuine and gracious service. A memorable experience awaits every guest. Just blocks from the financial district, the hotel is centrally located within downtown for convenient access to shopping, dining and entertainment. Richmond Int'l. Airport: 9 miles/16 km, 15 minutes.

Worldwide Reservations
www.preferredhotels.com
+800 323 7500 USA/Canada
+00 800 3237 5001 Europe (UIFN)
Other areas: See page 204

107

KINGSMILL RESORT & SPA

Contemporary architecture and furnishings welcome guests to this immaculately landscaped setting situated along Virginia's historic James River. Water views provide a relaxing backdrop to golf, tennis and other resort activities. Set on 3,000 acres (1,214 hectares) of woodlands overlooking the James River in Williamsburg, Virginia. Williamsburg/Newport News Int'l. Airport: 12 miles/19 km, 20 minutes.

ACCOMMODATIONS: 400 total guestrooms, including 185 suites, with all villa-style guestrooms and suites offering river, golf and tennis views. Some feature full kitchens and living rooms with fireplaces.

FACILITIES/SERVICES: 63 holes of golf, The Spa at Kingsmill, 15 tennis courts, Sports Club, two pools, ball courts, fitness center, marina and seasonal children's program.

BUSINESS SERVICES: Conference concierge for each meeting, continuous break service and on-site Business Center with T-1 Internet access.

DINING: Five restaurants and lounges, including "Eagles," an authentic steak and chop house featuring Kingsmill's exclusive beech-wood-smoked cooking and an extensive selection of fine wines.

MEETINGS: Total Meeting Rooms: 16 Total Sq. Ft.: 16,000 / Sq. M.: 1,490

RATES: USD 129.00 to 937.00; Group, Package rates.

Mr. Joseph Durante III, Executive Vice President & Managing Director

1010 Kingsmill Road
Williamsburg, Virginia 23185, USA
Tel: +1 757 253 1703
Fax: +1 757 253 8237
Email: reservations@kingsmill.com
www.kingsmill.com

Worldwide Reservations
www.preferredhotels.com
+800 323 7500 USA/Canada
+00 800 3237 5001 Europe (UIFN)
Other areas: See page 204

SORRENTO HOTEL

Seattle, Washington, USA

ACCOMMODATIONS: 76 total guestrooms, including 42 suites, each with data port, voice mail, stereos with CD players, robes, mini-bar, complimentary high-speed Internet access, cordless phones, 400-thread-count linens and pillow-top mattresses.

FACILITIES/SERVICES: Nautilus exercise center, babysitting, dry cleaning, shoe shine, salon, town car service and concierge.

BUSINESS SERVICES: Business Center and complimentary high-speed Internet access.

DINING: "Hunt Club" serves regional Northwest and Mediterranean cuisine. "Fireside Room" features cocktails, light menu and entertainment. "Piazza Capri" offers seasonal dining alfresco.

MEETINGS: Total Meeting Rooms: 4 Total Sq. Ft.: 4,000 / Sq. M.: 372

RATES: USD 275.00 to 2,700.00; Corporate, Group, Package rates.

Mr. Stan Kott,
Vice President & Managing Director

900 Madison Street
Seattle, Washington 98104, USA
Tel: +1 206 622 6400
Fax: +1 206 343 6155
Email: mail@hotelsorrento.com
www.hotelsorrento.com

Gracing the city with its breathtaking Italianate architecture for nearly a century, the Sorrento is a stylish oasis and one of Seattle's most recognizable and cherished landmarks. Overlooking the downtown skyline, Puget Sound and the Olympic Mountains, the hotel offers rich décor, casual elegance and Mediterranean-inspired cuisine and ambiance. Convenient to financial, medical and shopping districts. Seattle-Tacoma Int'l. Airport: 14 miles/ 23 km, 25 minutes.

Worldwide Reservations
www.preferredhotels.com
+800 323 7500   USA/Canada
+00 800 3237 5001   Europe (UIFN)
Other areas: See page 204

THE WOODMARK HOTEL ON LAKE WASHINGTON

The luxury of this lakeside retreat and world-class spa embraces travelers with the charm of a private residence. Combining intimacy and elegance, The Woodmark showcases shoreline views of the Seattle skyline and Olympic Mountains, and is the only hotel located on the shores of Lake Washingon, 20 minutes east of Seattle. Prominently set within a waterfront community, minutes from shopping, galleries, the high-tech corridors of Redmond/Bellevue and tourist destinations. Seattle-Tacoma Int'l. Airport: 18 miles/30 km, 30 minutes.

ACCOMMODATIONS: 100 total guestrooms, including 21 suites, each with Internet access, voice mail, data port, newspaper, CD player, safe, robes, hair dryer and mini-bar. Many with balcony and lake views.

FACILITIES/SERVICES: Spa treatments, plush bedding and pillow selection, concierge, shoe shine, child care services, salon, dry cleaning, shops and travel agency. Complimentary amenities: tours of Lake Washington aboard the Woodmark II, Internet access, late-night snacks and fitness center.

BUSINESS SERVICES: Airline ticketing, secretarial and translating services.

DINING: "Waters Lakeside Bistro" for Northwest cuisine, "Cucina Carillon Point" for Italian, "Yarrow Bay Beach Café & Grill" for seafood and "The Library Bar" for afternoon tea and libations.

MEETINGS: Total Meeting Rooms: 7 Total Sq. Ft.: 5,076 / Sq. M.: 473

RATES: USD 215.00 to 1,800.00; Corporate, Group, Package rates.

Mr. Marc Nowak, General Manager

1200 Carillon Point
Kirkland, Washington 98033, USA
Tel: +1 425 822 3700
Fax: +1 425 822 3699
Email: mail@thewoodmark.com
www.thewoodmark.com

Worldwide Reservations

www.preferredhotels.com
+800 323 7500 USA/Canada
+00 800 3237 5001 Europe (UIFN)
Other areas: See page 204

WILLOWS LODGE

ACCOMMODATIONS: 86 total guestrooms, including 6 suites, most with garden views. Extensive woodwork, stone fireplaces, quality beds with down duvets and linens by Frette, CD/DVD systems, patios, customized mini-bar, complimentary high-speed Internet access, voice mail and robes.

FACILITIES/SERVICES: The Challenge Course at Willows Lodge...for the development of organizational teambuilding skills, full service spa, fitness center, Jacuzzi and sauna.

BUSINESS SERVICES: Business and concierge services. Complimentary Internet access in guestrooms.

DINING: Two of the best in the Northwest, "The Herbfarm," renowned as one of America's finest dining establishments. The "Barking Frog" features the freshest local ingredients. Seasonal alfresco-style dining in the courtyard.

MEETINGS: Total Meeting Rooms: 6 Total Sq. Ft.: 5,153 / Sq. M.: 480

RATES: USD 260.00 to 750.00; Corporate, Group, Package rates.

Mr. James Simkins, General Manager

14580 Northeast 145th Street
Woodinville, Washington 98072, USA
Tel: +1 425 424 3900
Fax: +1 425 424 2585
Email: mail@willowslodge.com
www.willowslodge.com

Rural and rustic in ambiance, Willows Lodge is one of the latest entries into greater Seattle's collection of luxury lodgings and spas. This 86-room, Northwest-style lodge is situated in Woodinville on five exquisitely landscaped acres (2 hectares) that border the Sammamish River in the heart of Woodinville wine country. Adjacent to Chateau Ste. Michelle and Columbia Wineries, Redhook Brewery and close to the Silicon Forest of the Pacific Northwest. Seattle-Tacoma Int'l. Airport: 35 miles/56 km, 45 minutes.

Worldwide Reservations
www.preferredhotels.com
+800 323 7500 USA/Canada
+00 800 3237 5001 Europe (UIFN)
Other areas: See page 204

111

THE PFISTER HOTEL

Built in 1893 as a "palace for the people," The Pfister contains the largest collection of Victorian art of its kind in the world. The Pfister offers luxurious hospitality in the heart of downtown Milwaukee. In the exclusive East Town neighborhood, three blocks from Lake Michigan, close to the Milwaukee Art Museum, convention center, shopping and entertainment. Mitchell Int'l. Airport: 12 miles/19 km, 15 minutes.

ACCOMMODATIONS: 307 total guestrooms, including 82 suites, each with two phones, data port, voice mail, newspaper, safe, in-room coffee makers and mini-bar. VCR and fax on request.

FACILITIES/SERVICES: 24-hour room service, concierge, dry cleaning, shoe shine, salon, florist, shops, fitness center and indoor pool.

BUSINESS SERVICES: Secretarial services available.

DINING: "Celia" for fine dining, "Café at the Pfister" for contemporary cuisine, "Café Rouge" for champagne brunch and luncheon buffet, the "Lobby Lounge" for afternoon tea, cocktails and entertainment, and "Blu," an upscale, intimate lounge located atop the Pfister tower.

MEETINGS: Total Meeting Rooms: 18 Total Sq. Ft.: 25,000 / Sq. M.: 2,328

RATES: USD 189.00 to 990.00; Corporate, Group, Package rates.

Mr. John D. Williams,
General Manager

424 East Wisconsin Avenue
Milwaukee, Wisconsin 53202, USA
Tel: +1 414 273 8222
Fax: +1 414 273 5025
Email: info@thepfisterhotel.com
www.thepfisterhotel.com

Worldwide Reservations

www.preferredhotels.com
+800 323 7500 USA/Canada
+00 800 3237 5001 Europe (UIFN)
Other areas: See page 204

It's Time to Celebrate!

Uncork the champagne, let the bubbly flow. At Preferred hotels and resorts, celebrate that special occasion with luxury and unsurpassed service.

SNAKE RIVER LODGE & SPA

ACCOMMODATIONS: 133 total guestrooms, including 45 suites, each with two multi-line phones, voice mail, data port, Internet access, newspaper, safe, robes, hair dryer and refrigerator.

FACILITIES/SERVICES: Avanyu Spa, concierge, fitness center, salon and shopping. In winter, skiing, ice-skating, dog-sledding and cross-country skiing. In summer, fly-fishing school, mountain biking, hiking, tram and horseback riding. Golf nearby.

BUSINESS SERVICES: On-site business services available.

DINING: Snake River Lodge & Spa's popular "GameFish Restaurant" features New American cuisine with a Western Flair and serves breakfast, lunch and dinner daily.

MEETINGS: Total Meeting Rooms: 4 Total Sq. Ft.: 4,041 / Sq. M.: 376

RATES: USD 150.00 to 1,500.00; Group, Package rates.

Mr. Bruce Grosbety,
General Manager

7710 Granite Loop Road, P.O. Box 348
Jackson Hole, Wyoming 83025, USA
Tel: +1 307 732 6000
Fax: +1 307 732 6009
Email: info@snakeriverlodge.com
www.rockresorts.com

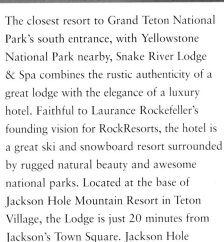

The closest resort to Grand Teton National Park's south entrance, with Yellowstone National Park nearby, Snake River Lodge & Spa combines the rustic authenticity of a great lodge with the elegance of a luxury hotel. Faithful to Laurance Rockefeller's founding vision for RockResorts, the hotel is a great ski and snowboard resort surrounded by rugged natural beauty and awesome national parks. Located at the base of Jackson Hole Mountain Resort in Teton Village, the Lodge is just 20 minutes from Jackson's Town Square. Jackson Hole Airport: 20 miles/32 km, 25 minutes.

Worldwide Reservations
www.preferredhotels.com
+800 323 7500 USA/Canada
+00 800 3237 5001 Europe (UIFN)
Other areas: See page 204

Latin America
& The Caribbean

SANDY LANE

The resort, which recently underwent major reconstruction and expansion, is set in an ancient mahogany grove overlooking a gorgeous crescent of beach on Barbados' western coast. The architecture is classical Palladian style, like the original building, and the hotel features a luxurious white coral stone rotunda, Italian marble floors, plantation-style furniture and sumptuous décor. Located along the west coast of Barbados, this luxury resort is 8 miles/ 13 km. from Bridgetown. Grantley Adams Int'l. Airport: 8 miles/13 km, 30 minutes.

ACCOMMODATIONS: 112 total guestrooms, including 18 suites, each with two phones, data port, voice mail, fax machine, newspaper, CD player, safe, mini-bar, robes and hair dryer.

FACILITIES/SERVICES: Spa, concierge services, shoe shine, fitness center, child care services, salon, tennis, dry cleaning, florist, shops, children's center, golf and water sports.

BUSINESS SERVICES: On-site Business Center.

DINING: "Bajan Blue Restaurant" offers all-day dining featuring Mediterranean and Caribbean cuisine. "L'Acajou Restaurant" features an eclectic mix of Carib-Asian and French influence cuisine.

MEETINGS: Total Meeting Rooms: 6 Total Sq. Ft.: 8,000 / Sq. M.: 745

RATES: USD 600.00 to 6,500.00; Group rates.

Mr. Colm Hannon, General Manager

St. James , Barbados
Tel: +1 246 444 2000
Fax: +1 246 444 2222
Email: mail@sandylane.com
www.sandylane.com

Worldwide Reservations
www.preferredhotels.com
+800 323 7500 USA/Canada
+00 800 3237 5001 Europe (UIFN)
Other areas: See page 204

PETER ISLAND RESORT

Tortola, British Virgin Islands

ACCOMMODATIONS: 56 accommodations, 52 total guestrooms, including 20 suites, and 4 luxury villa estates, each with phones, data port, voice mail, CD/clock radio, safe, mini-bar, refrigerator and robes.

FACILITIES/SERVICES: All non-motorized water sports and instruction are complimentary as well as fitness center, tennis courts, hiking trails, horticulture tours, library and yacht service to and from Tortola. Full service spa and dive shop are available at a fee.

DINING: "Tradewinds" prepares West Indian dishes and continental classics. "Wine Room," "Deadman's Beach Bar & Grill," "Drakes Channel Lounge" and "White Bay Picnic Lunch" also available.

MEETINGS: Total Meeting Rooms: 2 Total Sq. Ft.: 900 / Sq. M.: 84

RATES: USD 540.00 to 1,250.00; Group, Package rates.

Mr. Jeff Humes, General Manager

Box 211
Road Town, Tortola, British Virgin Islands
Tel: +1 770 476 9988
Fax: +1 770 476 4979
Email: reservations@peterisland.com
www.peterisland.com

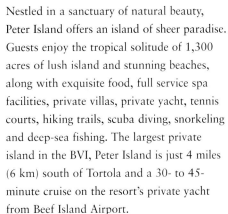

Nestled in a sanctuary of natural beauty, Peter Island offers an island of sheer paradise. Guests enjoy the tropical solitude of 1,300 acres of lush island and stunning beaches, along with exquisite food, full service spa facilities, private villas, private yacht, tennis courts, hiking trails, scuba diving, snorkeling and deep-sea fishing. The largest private island in the BVI, Peter Island is just 4 miles (6 km) south of Tortola and a 30- to 45-minute cruise on the resort's private yacht from Beef Island Airport.

Worldwide Reservations
www.preferredhotels.com
+800 323 7500 USA/Canada
+00 800 3237 5001 Europe (UIFN)
Other areas: See page 204

119

SECRETS EXCELLENCE PUNTA CANA

Raising All-Inclusive to a new level of luxury, this lavish resort is perfect for the guest looking to be pampered. This all-suite resort is dedicated to serving adults and couples. Secrets Excellence offers superior amenities and services such as four-poster beds and Jacuzzi in every suite, fine dining, spa and wellness center, casino, and daytime and nighttime entertainment. Located one hour from Punta Cana Int'l. Airport, on a mile-long stretch of white sand beach, Secrets Excellence is splendid isolation.

Worldwide Reservations

www.preferredhotels.com
+800 323 7500 USA/Canada
+00 800 3237 5001 Europe (UIFN)
Other areas: See page 204

ACCOMMODATIONS: 446 suites, each offering Jacuzzi, balcony or terrace, mini-bar, color satellite TV and coffee maker. Guests staying in the Excellence Club receive VIP amenities and services such as private concierge, private lounge serving continental breakfast and afternoon hors d'oeuvres, upgraded room amenities, daily newspaper, slippers and bathrobes, and pillow menu.

FACILITIES/SERVICES: Cascade pool and lagoon pool, spa, fitness center, horseback riding, bicycling, tennis, squash, casino, sailing, snorkeling, Jacuzzi.

BUSINESS SERVICES: Audio/video equipment rental, computer with Internet access, and photocopy service available.

DINING: 7 à la carte and one buffet restaurant offering Italian, Tex-Mex, Mediterranean, Caribbean, seafood, Mexican, Oriental and Continental cuisine; 9 bars and 24-hour room service available.

MEETINGS: Total Meeting Rooms: Total Sq. Ft.: 2,605 / Sq. M.: 242

RATES: USD 300.00 to 966.00; Corporate, Group, Package rates.

Mr. Emilio Huhn, General Manager

Playas Uvero Alto
La Altagracia, Dominican Republic
Tel: +1 809 685 9880
Fax: +1 809 685 9990
Email: e.huhn@secretsresorts.com.do
www.secretsresorts.com

One of the finest beaches in Acapulco belongs to the Quinta Real Acapulco — an exclusive boutique resort hotel with fabulous facilities. With sailing, diving, fishing, parasailing, golf, dancing, music and dining, it is little wonder that the Quinta Real is fast becoming the place to be. Perfectly located overlooking the Pacific Ocean, on prestigious Punta Diamante, 15 minutes from all the activity of the Golden Zone of Acapulco. Acapulco Int'l. Airport: 6 mi/10 km, 10 min.

Acapulco, Mexico

ACCOMMODATIONS: 74 luxurious Master and Grand Class Suites with marble floors and color satellite TV. 6 Governor Suites and one Presidential Suite available, each with Jacuzzi and its own private pool.

FACILITIES/SERVICES: The hotel boasts an exclusive Beach Club with 'infinity' pool, spa, fitness room, pool bar and Acapulco's finest beach. A comprehensive range of water sports is available and an excellent golf course is located nearby. Numerous shopping and dining options are available in Acapulco's Golden Zone.

BUSINESS SERVICES: The hotel can provide a full range of secretarial services.

DINING: A fabulous hilltop restaurant serves Mexican specialties and international favorites with stunning views over the Pacific Ocean. The poolside bar serves lighter fare.

MEETINGS: Total Meeting Rooms: 2 Total Sq. Ft.: 2,634 / Sq. M.: 245

RATES: USD from 200.00; Corporate, Group, Package rates.

Mr. Juan Riba, General Manager

Paseo de la Quinta, Lote #6,
Desarrollo Turistico Real, Diamante
Acapulco 39907, Mexico
Tel: +52 744 469 1500
Fax: +52 744 469 1540
Email: ventas-aca@quinta-real.com
www.quintareal.com

QUINTA REAL AGUASCALIENTES

Constructed in the style of a traditional monastery complete with a stone façade, bell tower and arched walkways, Quinta Real Aguascalientes does indeed provide an atmosphere of almost monastic tranquillity. As you relax beside the cool, cobalt-blue swimming pool, you can almost hear the ancient bell calling the faithful to prayer. The hotel is situated only 4 km from the historic center of Aguascalientes and 8 km from the main commercial district with stores and restaurants. Aguascalientes Int'l. Jesús Terán Airport is 28 km away (20 min by taxi).

ACCOMMODATIONS: 85 lavish suites, each with mini-bar, PC connection point, color cable TV, complimentary newspaper, sound-proofing, temperature control, robe and turndown service.

FACILITIES/SERVICES: Heated outdoor swimming pool surrounded by beautiful gardens. Tours of San Marcos winery can also be arranged.

BUSINESS SERVICES: Business Center and secretarial services.

DINING: "Los Murales" Restaurant is named after its lovely painted murals by artists from Guadalajara and it features many regional specialities.

MEETINGS: Total Meeting Rooms: 4 Total Sq. Ft.: 6,101 / Sq. M.: 568

RATES: USD from 175.00; Corporate, Group, Package rates.

Ms. Gloria Liceaga, General Manager

Ave. Aguascalientes Sur 601,
Col. Jardines de la Asuncion
Aguascalientes 20070, Mexico
Tel: +52 499 978 5818
Fax: +52 499 978 5616
Email: reser-ags@quintareal.com
www.quintareal.com

Worldwide Reservations
www.preferredhotels.com
+800 323 7500   USA/Canada
+00 800 3237 5001   Europe (UIFN)
Other areas: See page 204

ACCOMMODATIONS: Master Suites, 25 Grand Suites and a Presidential Suite each with traditional Mexican furniture and art, stone fireplaces, marble bathrooms, CD player, TV and VCR, as well as a hair dryer and bathrobes.

FACILITIES/SERVICES: Pool, whirlpool and excursions to Tlaquepaque, Tonala and Ajijic available. Mexico's largest lake, Lake Chapala, shopping and golf are nearby.

BUSINESS SERVICES: Business Center with a computer and fax.

DINING: Mexican and international cuisine can be enjoyed in the privacy of your suite, beside the pool or in the elegant restaurant.

MEETINGS: Total Meeting Rooms: 2 Total Sq. Ft.: 8,034 / Sq. M.: 748

RATES: USD from 240.00; Corporate, Group, Package rates.

Mr. Alfredo Aguilar, General Manager

@

Ave. Mexico 2727, Col. Monreaz
Guadalajara 44680, Mexico
Tel: +52 33 3669 0600
Fax: +52 33 3669 0634
Email: reserv-gdl@quintareal.com
www.quintareal.com

Only in Guadalajara could you find a hotel so richly infused with native color. The handiwork of Mexican's finest craftsmen is found throughout the Quinta Real Guadalajara, a boutique hotel with elegant period furniture, stuccoed ceilings and impressive art. You will be hard put to find a more authentic and welcoming place to stay in this most Mexican of cities. The hotel is situated in the city's premier West End residential zone providing quick and easy access to anywhere in the city. Miguel Hidalgo Int'l. Airport is 20 km away (30 min by car).

Worldwide Reservations
www.preferredhotels.com
+800 323 7500 USA/Canada
+00 800 3237 5001 Europe (UIFN)
Other areas: See page 204

QUINTA REAL CASA DE SIERRA NEVADA

Built in 1580, the Casa de Sierra Nevada is one of Mexico's finest hotels. A few blocks from the town square on a cobblestone street, this hotel comprises beautiful colonial houses, all with hand-painted tiles and colonial furnishings. Enjoy horse riding at the nearby La Loma Ranch, take a dip in the pool or simply relax in the courtyard. Experience this haven, and you won't want to leave. Located in the center of Mexico, Guanajuato is part of the historic route of Mexican independence. The Guanajuato Int'l. Airport is a 1 hour drive and Mexico City Airport is 175 miles away (3 hours).

ACCOMMODATIONS: Colonial mansions house 33 suites, each with colonial décor, seating areas, fireplaces and hand-painted tile baths. Some rooms face onto courtyards and gardens, while others have balconies and beautiful views.

FACILITIES/SERVICES: Pool and spa services. Just 10 minutes from the hotel is the 300-acre La Loma Ranch for horse riding.

BUSINESS SERVICES: Business services available on request.

DINING: Award-winning "Del Centro" has fine cuisine. "Restaurant Sierra Nevada" has Mexican fare in the park. The Lobby Bar "Casa del Parque" serves drinks with live music.

MEETINGS: Total Meeting Rooms: 1 Total Sq. Ft.: 243 / Sq. M.: 23

RATES: USD from 145.00; Corporate, Group, Package rates.

Mr. Umberto Roma, General Manager

Hospicio #35, San Miguel de Allende Guanajuato, 37700, Mexico
Tel: +52 415 152 7040
Fax: +52 415 152 1436
Email: sierranevada@quinta-real.com
www.quintareal.com

Worldwide Reservations
www.preferredhotels.com
+800 323 7500 USA/Canada
+00 800 3237 5001 Europe (UIFN)
Other areas: See page 204

QUINTA REAL HUATULCO

ACCOMMODATIONS: 27 suites each with traditional décor and furnishings, views of Tangolunda Bay and Jacuzzi. 1 Presidential Suite, 6 Master Suites and 20 Grand Class suites, some of which have their own private swimming pools.

FACILITIES/SERVICES: Private beach, beach club with 2 swimming pools and 1 tennis court, golf nearby, bicycle/motorcycle trips, rafting, walking, horse riding and tours of a coffee plantation and the 9 bays.

BUSINESS SERVICES: Business services available on request.

DINING: A gourmet restaurant serves Mexican specialties and international favorites overlooking the Pacific Ocean. Cocktails available in the atmospheric bar and lunch is served alfresco at the "Beach Club" restaurant.

MEETINGS: Total Meeting Rooms: 1 Total Sq. Ft.: 646 / Sq. M.: 60

RATES: USD from 200.00; Corporate, Group, Package rates.

Mr. Federico Roth, General Manager

Paseo Benito Juarez 2, Zona Hotelera, Bahias
Huatulco 70989, Mexico
Tel: +52 958 581 0428
Fax: +52 958 581 0429
Email: jrecepcion-hux@quintareal.com
www.quintareal.com

The Bay of Tangolunda provides a secluded and romantic setting for Quinta Real Huatulco on Mexico's Pacific Coast. Set against a backdrop of jungle, this intimate hotel combines the natural beauty of stunning beaches, blue seas and exotic gardens. For the ultimate in luxury, you may prefer a suite with your own private pool. The hotel is located in Tangolunda Bay, one of the most beautiful of the 9 Huatulco bays, with 30 km of beaches and a backdrop of rivers, mountains, hillsides and valleys. Huatulco Int'l. Airport is 25 km away (35 min by taxi).

Worldwide Reservations
www.preferredhotels.com
+800 323 7500 USA/Canada
+00 800 3237 5001 Europe (UIFN)
Other areas: See page 204

QUINTA REAL MONTERREY

Set against the backdrop of mountains that surround this lively city, the Quinta Real Monterrey is a haven of elegance and tranquillity. Renowned as being the most refined address in town, this hotel features a central courtyard, stunning cupola and colorful murals. Queen Anne chairs and bouquets of flowers promote a club-like atmosphere. In the best quarter of the industrial capital of Mexico, near the business district and 15 min from the Cintermex Expo and Fair Center. Mariano Escobedo Airport is 30 km away (45 min by taxi).

ACCOMMODATIONS: 165 lovely suites each with canopied beds, air conditioning, mini-bar and PC connection point. The new Executive Tower has large, modern luxury suites and an efficient full-service Executive Center.

FACILITIES/SERVICES: Fitness center, steam room and sauna. Tennis, golf, shopping and horse riding nearby. Nearby excursions include beer tasting at the Cuautemoc Brewery, or tours of the elegant Kristaluxus crystal factory.

BUSINESS SERVICES: A fully equipped Business Center.

DINING: A fine gourmet restaurant offers Mexican and international cuisine. The bar offers lively Mexican music nightly.

MEETINGS: Total Meeting Rooms: 4 Total Sq. Ft.: 3,788 / Sq. M.: 353

RATES: USD from 210.00; Corporate, Group, Package rates.

Mr. Marco Antonio Cantoral, General Manager

@

Diego Rivera 500, Fracc. Valle Oriente Monterrey 66260, Mexico
Tel: +52 818 368 1000
Fax: +52 818 368 1070
Email: sgarcia@quintareal.com
www.quintareal.com

Worldwide Reservations
www.preferredhotels.com
+800 323 7500   USA/Canada
+00 800 3237 5001   Europe (UIFN)
Other areas: See page 204

QUINTA REAL PUERTO VALLARTA

ACCOMMODATIONS: 67 spacious suites each with the finest in Mexican décor. Special Grand Class suites have their own private plunge pool as well as a Jacuzzi.

FACILITIES/SERVICES: Tennis courts, fitness center with yoga and t'ai chi classes, golf, library, pool and spa. The marina area, with restaurants, shops and galleries, is a 5-minute walk, and beautiful local beaches are nearby.

BUSINESS SERVICES: Business services available on request.

DINING: "El Candil" serves the finest international and Mexican cuisine. The open-air snack bar, "Hoyo 19", offers healthy alternatives. The oceanfront Beach Club has a delicious casual menu.

MEETINGS: Total Meeting Rooms: 1 Total Sq. Ft.: 775 / Sq. M.: 72

RATES: USD from 250.00; Corporate, Group, Package rates.

Mr. Bernard Mercier,
General Manager

Pelicanos #311, Fracc. Marina Vallarta
Puerto Vallarta 48354, Mexico
Tel: +52 322 226 6688
Fax: +52 322 226 6699
Email: jbecerra@quintareal.com
www.quintareal.com

Nestled within a golf course, Quinta Real Puerto Vallarta is a peaceful oasis. Located in Marina Vallarta with beaches and palm-covered mountains nearby, the hotel with its beach club and spa is a private retreat with personalized service. Luxurious décor, tropical gardens and private plunge pools create a picturesque haven. In the heart of Marina Vallarta golf course, the hotel is just a few minutes walk from the marina and 15 minutes from downtown and El Malecon, the boardwalk. Puerto Vallarta's Int'l. Airport, Gustavo Diaz Ordaz, is 5 minutes away.

Worldwide Reservations
www.preferredhotels.com
+800 323 7500 USA/Canada
+00 800 3237 5001 Europe (UIFN)
Other areas: See page 204

127

SECRETS CAPRI RIVIERA CANCUN

Dedicated to serving adults and couples, Secrets Capri Riviera Cancun embodies romance. Expressing the generous soul of Mexico and commanding a pristine beachfront location between Playa del Carmen and Cancun, Secrets Capri Riviera Cancun is a luxury oasis that embraces the elegance of traditional Mexican design and ensures unmatched standards of all-inclusive service and pampering. Nestled in 71 tropical acres and surrounded by endless white beaches, the crystal-clear Caribbean Sea and historic Mayan ruins. Exciting Playa del Carmen is only 5 minutes, 5 kms/7 miles away. Cancun Int'l. Airport: 20 miles/33 km, 40 minutes.

Worldwide Reservations

www.preferredhotels.com

+800 323 7500 USA/Canada

+00 800 3237 5001 Europe (UIFN)

Other areas: See page 204

ACCOMMODATIONS: 287 total guestrooms, majority of rooms with ocean view, including 86 junior suites and four Presidential Suites, each featuring private balcony, marble bathroom with whirlpool tub and separate shower, CD/DVD player, mini-bar, coffee/tea maker, newspaper and data ports.

FACILITIES/SERVICES: World class spa and spa garden, fitness center, pool, Jacuzzi, land and water sports, fitness trail, championship golf nearby, library, billiards, salon and dry cleaning.

BUSINESS SERVICES: Business Center and secretarial/translating services.

DINING: Four gourmet, and one buffet restaurant offering Mediterranean, Pan-Asian, seafood, Mexican and Continental cuisines. Beach bar and grill, pool bar.

MEETINGS: Total Meeting Rooms: 5 Total Sq. Ft.: 8,400 / Sq. M.: 782

RATES: USD 334.00 to 1100.00; Corporate, Group, Package rates. Rates are all-inclusive of all meals, premium beverages, sports activities and entertainment.

Mr. Robert Noe, General Manager

Carretera Chetumal - Puerto Juarez Km. 299
Playa del Carmen, Riviera Maya c.p. 77711, Mexico
Tel: +52 984 873 4880
Fax: +52 984 873 4881
Email: info@secretsresorts.com
www.secretsresorts.com

SECRETS EXCELLENCE RIVIERA CANCUN

ACCOMMODATIONS: 442 all-suite guest accommodations offer deluxe and junior suites, honeymoon and swim-out suites each offering at least one Jacuzzi, marble bathrooms, private balcony or terrace. Satellite TV, mini-bar refreshed daily and newspaper. Excellence Club VIP section offers upgraded amenities and oceanfront suites.

FACILITIES/SERVICES: Six meandering pools, an amazing spa and spa garden, fitness center, 3 outdoor Jacuzzis, tennis, bicycling, daytime and night-time entertainment, non-motorized water sports.

BUSINESS SERVICES: Business Center with fax, Internet, photocopy, and meeting facilities.

DINING: Choice of 6 restaurants, featuring Continental, Mexican, Japanese, Steak & Seafood, and Gourmet cuisines; 9 bars.

MEETINGS: Total Meeting Rooms: 3 Total Sq. Ft.: 6,458 / Sq. M.: 600

RATES: USD 380.00 to 1760.00; Corporate, Group, Package rates.

Lote 1, Manzana 7, Supermanzana 11
Riviera Maya, Quintana Roo, Mexico
Email: info@secretsresorts.com
www.secretsresorts.com

Seekers of romantic seclusion and the excitement of Playa del Carmen and Cancun may now find both in this new luxury all-suite resort. This luxurious all-inclusive resort combines Caribbean and Mexican architecture with superior amenities. Perfect for singles, couples, honeymooners, weddings and guests who wish to be pampered. Located just 30 minutes south of Cancun and situated on a magnificent stretch of white-sand beach in the Riviera Maya.

Worldwide Reservations
www.preferredhotels.com
+800 323 7500   USA/Canada
+00 800 3237 5001   Europe (UIFN)
Other areas: See page 204

QUINTA REAL ZACATECAS

One of the world's most unusual hotels, the Quinta Real Zacatecas encircles the 17th-century San Pedro bullring. Blending the luxury of a modern hotel with the splendor of colonial architecture, the hotel faces the city's ancient arched viaduct. Located only half a mile from the city center and overlooking Sierra de Alica Park. The cathedral and museum are close by. Zacatecas Int'l. (Leobardo C. Ruiz) Airport is 29 km away (20–30 min by taxi).

ACCOMMODATIONS: 49 suites each with a bed recessed under a stone or wooden arch, air-conditioning, cable TV and mini-bar. Some suites with balcony and Jacuzzis.

FACILITIES/SERVICES: Swimming, fitness center, tennis, horse riding and golf are all available. Theaters, museums, shops and the cathedral of Zacatecas are nearby.

BUSINESS SERVICES: Secretarial services available for guests.

DINING: Overlooking the bullring, the hotel provides the setting for a memorable dining experience. Mexican and international cuisine at "La Plaza". "El Botarel" bar features live music.

MEETINGS: Total Meeting Rooms: 3 Total Sq. Ft.: 3,099 / Sq. M.: 289

RATES: USD from 145.00; Corporate, Group, Package rates.

Mr. Carlos Rocha, General Manager

Ave. Gonzalez Ortega, Colonia Centro
Zacatecas 98000, Mexico
Tel: +52 492 922 9104
Fax: +52 492 922 8440
Email: ventas-zac@quintareal.com
www.quintareal.com

Worldwide Reservations
www.preferredhotels.com
+800 323 7500 USA/Canada
+00 800 3237 5001 Europe (UIFN)
Other areas: See page 204

ISN'T IT TIME YOU INDULGED IN A LITTLE PREFERENTIAL TREATMENT WITH A *RESORT PERKS* PACKAGE FROM PREFERRED?

From stress-chasing hot stone massages to exquisite dining courtesy of our world-renowned chefs, *Preferred Resort Perks* have you covered from head to toe. Come and indulge yourself at one of the most distinctive, exclusive resorts in the world, each with its own special way of lavishing you with the sumptuous experiences and tactile treatments you desire most. From January 1–December 31, 2004, participating hotels are offering one of the following *Resort Perks*:

- Complimentary breakfast for two and parking
- Complimentary round of golf for two
- $100 USD Spa Credit

For more information and to book a *Preferred Resort Perks* package, please visit our Web site at www.preferredhotels.com/offers, contact your travel professional or call 1 800 323 7500.

PREFERRED
HOTELS & RESORTS
WORLD WIDE

Europe

ACCOMMODATIONS: 177 total guestrooms, including 35 suites, some with outdoor pool or whirlpool, direct-dial phone, mini-bar, safe, robes, hair dryer and satellite TV. CD player and VCR in all suites. Fax machine upon request.

FACILITIES/SERVICES: Tennis, squash, water sports, outdoor and indoor pools, thalassotherapy, spa, concierge, child care services and children's club, dry cleaning, shoe shine, salon, wine tasting, Jeep safaris, boat trips.

BUSINESS SERVICES: Translating and secretarial services available.

DINING: Each of Anassa's four restaurants, as well as the all-day dining facilities by the pools, offer a scrumptious choice of local and international dishes, using fresh produce from the hotel's own farm.

MEETINGS: Total Meeting Rooms: 3 Total Sq. Ft.: 10,680 / Sq. M.: 994

RATES: CYP 130.00 to 1,950.00; Corporate, Group, Package rates.

Mr. York Brandes, General Manager

P.O. Box 66006
CY8830 Polis, Cyprus
Tel: +357 2 688 8000
Fax: +357 2 632 2900
Email: anassa@thanoshotels.com

Anassa's architecture reflects the many aspects of Cyprus' history, with Greek and Roman mosaics and Venetian frescoes. Breathtaking views of the Mediterranean, stunning beaches and cool courtyards make this inviting resort a relaxing hideaway. West of the village of Neo Chorion, overlooking the wild beauty of the Akamas Peninsula, Anassa lies in the unspoiled and largely undiscovered region of Polis. Pafos Int'l. Airport: 31 miles/50 km, 45 minutes.

Worldwide Reservations
www.preferredhotels.com
+800 323 7500   USA/Canada
+00 800 3237 5001   Europe (UIFN)
Other areas: See page 204

THE ANNABELLE

ACCOMMODATIONS: 218 guestrooms, including 6 suites, 20 studio suites and 11 garden studio suites, each with mini-bar, direct-dial phone, radio, safe, robes and pay satellite TV. Some feature private Jacuzzi or splash pool, CD player and VCR. Fax machines upon request.

FACILITIES/SERVICES: Pools, health and beauty center, tennis court, squash, water sports, children's club, dry cleaning, salon and wine tastings. Three golf courses nearby.

BUSINESS SERVICES: Translating and secretarial services available.

DINING: "Amorosa" for contemporary cuisine, "The Mediterraneo" for Cypriot and Mediterranean cuisine. "Fontana" hosts theme evenings. The "Lobby Bar" features classical music.

MEETINGS: Total Meeting Rooms: 5 Total Sq. Ft.: 7,158 / Sq. M.: 666

RATES: CYP 72.00 to 960.00; Corporate, Group, Package rates.

Mr. Clive Bennett, General Manager

Poseidonos Avenue
Pafos 8102, Cyprus
Tel: +357 26 938 333
Fax: +357 26 945 502
Email: the-annabelle@thanoshotels.com
www.thanoshotels.com
res-annabelle@thanoshotels.com

From the elegant wood and marble of the lobby to the classical decorations and Greek statues of the ballroom, The Annabelle's interiors are utterly peaceful. Set on 6 acres (2 hectares) of lush tropical gardens overlooking the bay and notable archeological sites, The Annabelle treats guests to the genuine friendliness of a family-run hotel. On the southwest coast of Cyprus in Pafos, the birthplace of Aphrodite. Pafos Int'l. Airport: 10 miles/16 km, 15 minutes.

Worldwide Reservations
www.preferredhotels.com
+800 323 7500 USA/Canada
+00 800 3237 5001 Europe (UIFN)
Other areas: See page 204

HOTEL PALACE PRAHA

Built in 1909 in Art Nouveau style, the hotel features an elegant façade and enchanting interior decoration. The Hotel Palace Praha prides itself on fostering a family atmosphere, offering impeccable personal service and the warmest of welcomes to every guest. Hotel Palace Praha is centrally located on the corner of Panská and Jindrisská streets, adjacent to the famous Wenceslav's Square and the Mustek subway station. Prague Ruzyne Airport: 11 miles/18 km, 30 minutes.

ACCOMMODATIONS: 124 luxury guestrooms, including 10 suites, each with audio/video equipment, two phones, voice mail, data port, in-room Internet access, trouser press, safe, mini-bar and tea/coffee facilities.

FACILITIES/SERVICES: In-house laundry and dry cleaning, exchange office, concierge, child care services, massage, salon, sauna, international newspapers and magazines.

BUSINESS SERVICES: On-site Business Service Center, conference center with state-of-the-art technical equipment.

DINING: "Restaurant L'Epoque" features breakfast. The "Gourmet Club Lounge" offers breakfast, lunch, dinner and cocktails. The "Gourmet Club Restaurant" offers a selection of local and international cuisine as well as a unique selection of wines from around the world.

MEETINGS: Total Meeting Rooms: 3 Total Sq. Ft.: 3,950 / Sq. M.: 368

RATES: EUR 295.00 to 1000.00; Corporate, Group, Package rates.

Mr. Josef F. Santin, General Manager

Panská 12
Prague I CZ-111 21, Czech Republic
Tel: +420 224 093 111
Fax: +420 224 221 240
Email: palhoprg@palacehotel.cz
www.palacehotel.cz

Worldwide Reservations
www.preferredhotels.com
+800 323 7500 USA/Canada
+00 800 3237 5001 Europe (UIFN)
Other areas: See page 204

ACCOMMODATIONS: 291 total guestrooms, including 20 suites, each with views of the sea or the pretty, half-timbered courtyard.

FACILITIES/SERVICES: Indoor heated pool, sauna, solarium, gymnasium, steam bath, and game room. Thalassotherapy, casino, theater, cinema, tennis, golf and sailing are nearby.

BUSINESS SERVICES: Business Center available nearby for guests.

DINING: "La Belle Epoque" serves breakfast, brunch and a musical dinner with seafood and regional cooking. "La Potinière" is a private salon for up to 50 guests. "La Cour Normande" is open during the summer. Children are VIPs with their very own restaurant, "La Fermette," and a playroom.

MEETINGS: Total Meeting Rooms: 19 Total Sq. Ft.: 6,208 / Sq. M.: 578

RATES: EUR 245.00 to 489.00; Corporate, Group, Package rates.

Mr. Gerard-Martial Laxenaire, General Manager

38 Rue Jean Mermoz
Deauville 14800, France
Tel: +33 23 198 6622
Fax: +33 23 198 6623
Email: gmlaxenaire@lucienbarriere.com
www.lucienbarriere.com

A seafront landmark since 1912, the Normandy Barrière is a grand hotel of singular charm. The façade of pale-green timber, whimsical turrets, dormer windows and interior courtyards of checkered stone contrast with sumptuous guestrooms, offering every modern comfort. The Normandy Barrière is located on the seafront adjacent to the casino and in the heart of the town center. Deauville St Gatien is 15 km away (10 minutes by car). Paris Charles de Gaulle Airport is 220 km away (2 hours by car).

LA TRÉMOILLE

Fully renovated in 2002, La Trémoille is located on Paris' Right Bank in the Haute Couture district. Set in a traditional Haussman building just off the River Seine and built in the 19th century, the hotel retains much of its original elegance with a subtle blend of traditional and contemporary styles. Ideally situated on a quiet street in the "Triangle d'Or," in the heart of the 8th Arrondissement, within walking distance of the Champs-Élysées, Arc de Triomphe, Eiffel Tower and the famous shops of the Avenue Montaigne. Paris Roissy-CDG Airport: 15 miles/25 km, 45 minutes.

Worldwide Reservations

www.preferredhotels.com
+800 323 7500 USA/Canada
+00 800 3237 5001 Europe (UIFN)
Other areas: See page 204

ACCOMMODATIONS: 93 total guestrooms, including 5 suites, each with multi-line phones, voice mail, data port, high-speed Internet access, wireless Internet access, video on demand, CD and DVD player, trouser press, safe and mini-bar.

FACILITIES/SERVICES: Concierge, shoe shine, dry cleaning, health club and fitness center.

BUSINESS SERVICES: Secretarial services available through concierge. Fax machines available in rooms upon request.

DINING: Our restaurant and bar. "Senso," designed and managed by Sir Terence Conran, offers traditional French cuisine in an exciting décor. Jazz atmosphere with live music in the "Senso Bar."

MEETINGS: Total Meeting Rooms: 2 Total Sq. Ft.: 646 / Sq. M.: 60

RATES: EUR 399.00 to 950.00; Corporate, Group, Package rates.

Mr. Pascal Dupuis, General Manager

14, rue de la Trémoille
Paris 75 008, France
Tel: +33 15 652 1400
Fax: +33 14 070 0108
Email: reservation@hotel-tremoille.com
www.hotel-tremoille.com

ACCOMMODATIONS: 56 total guestrooms, including 8 suites, contemporary or classic style, each featuring upscale and high-tech equipment (flat-screen TV, DVD and CD players), WIFI connection to Internet, 2 dual-lines phone with voice-mail, individual safe and mini-bar. Fully equipped marble bathroom.

FACILITIES/SERVICES: Same-day laundry and dry cleaning service, CD and DVD library, concierge, wireless high-speed Internet access (WIFI), valet service and parking.

BUSINESS SERVICES: Business Center available on request.

DINING: Watch Parisian life roll past from the outdoor dining terrace of the newly refurbished "Le Restaurant," open all day long around a new food and service concept. Or sit back and enjoy the latest cocktails by the open wood-burning fire of the "Library Bar."

MEETINGS: Total Meeting Rooms: 1 Total Sq. Ft.: 398 / Sq. M.: 37

RATES: EUR 290.00 to 1,130.00; Package rates.

Mr. Alexandre Fougerole,
General Manager

3 Rue de Montalembert
Paris 75007, France
Tel: +33 14 549 6868
Fax: +33 14 549 6949
Email: welcome@montalembert.com
www.montalembert.com

Montalembert recently unveiled a new look while maintaining the spirit of the original. The interior décor has been enriched by new materials and colors: white leather armchairs, grey velvet sofas, tobacco cream fabrics. Ideally located in the very heart of Paris, on the Left Bank, the Montalembert is situated near the crossroads of Rue Du Bac and Boulevard Saint-Germain. The location provides easy access to galleries, boutiques, cafes and antique shops of the Left Bank. The Louvre and the Musee d'Orsay are a short walk away. Paris Orly Airport: 11 miles/18 km, 30 minutes.

Worldwide Reservations
www.preferredhotels.com
+800 323 7500 USA/Canada
+00 800 3237 5001 Europe (UIFN)
Other areas: See page 204

HOTEL BAYERISCHER HOF

With more than 160 years of tradition, this historic hotel offers a variety of unique guestrooms and banqueting facilities. Located in the heart of Munich, it is among the grand hotels of the world. Across from the Frauenkirche Cathedral and an easy walk to business, shopping and cultural sites. Munich Int'l. Airport: 22 miles/35 km, 45 minutes.

ACCOMMODATIONS: 395 total guestrooms, including 58 suites, each individually decorated in different styles like colonial and country manor style. Two phones, data port, voice mail, Internet access, mini-bar, safe, robes and TV with Sony PlayStation. VCR on request.

FACILITIES/SERVICES: Indoor/outdoor pool, sun terrace, sauna, solarium, steam bath, massage, cardio fitness, salon, child care services, dry cleaning, concierge, theater, designer shops, kiosk and art gallery.

BUSINESS SERVICES: Business Center, secretarial and translating services.

DINING: Polynesian food and drinks at "Trader Vic's," international and regional cuisine at "Garden-Restaurant" with terrace, or Bavarian specialties in "Palais Keller."

MEETINGS: Total Meeting Rooms: 38 Total Sq. Ft.: 48,935 / Sq. M.: 4,437

RATES: EUR 212.00 to 1,450.00; Corporate, Group, Package rates.

Ms. Innegrit Volkhardt, Managing Owner

2-6 Promenadeplatz
Munich 80333, Germany
Tel: +49 892 1200
Fax: +49 89 212 0906
Email: info@bayerischerhof.de
www.bayerischerhof.de

Worldwide Reservations
www.preferredhotels.com
+800 323 7500 USA/Canada
+00 800 3237 5001 Europe (UIFN)
Other areas: See page 204

DROMOLAND CASTLE HOTEL

ACCOMMODATIONS: 100 total guestrooms, including 6 suites, each with phones, data port, voice mail, robes, slippers, complimentary Celtic Crossing liqueur, trouser press, iron & board, television, stereo, CDs, VCR (videos available from reception), safe, hair dryer and complimentary postcards.

FACILITIES/SERVICES: Pool, spa, fitness center, tennis, concierge, child care services, dry cleaning, shoe shine, salon, golf course and jogging trails.

BUSINESS SERVICES: Business Center, secretarial and translating services and complimentary Internet access.

DINING: Choose from "Earl of Thomond Restaurant" for gourmet dining or the brasserie-style "Fig Tree Restaurant."

MEETINGS: Total Meeting Rooms: 5 Total Sq. Ft.: 5,088 / Sq. M.: 474

RATES: EUR 215.00 to 1,245.00; Corporate, Group, Package rates.

Mr. Mark Nolan, General Manager

Newmarket-on-Fergus
County Clare, Ireland
Tel: +353 6 136 8144
Fax: +353 6 136 3355
Email: sales@dromoland.ie
www.dromoland.ie

This historic 16th-century castle was originally the stronghold of the High King of Ireland, Brian Boru. Nestled on 370 acres (150 hectares) of forest and parkland, and forted by its own private lake. The castle has a superb championship golf course, newly designed and reconstructed by the world-renowned golf course designer Ron Kirby in partnership with the legendary J.B. Carr. The course measures 6,850 yards and is a par 72. This majestic hotel is also warm and intimate, with log fires glowing throughout the public areas. Six miles (10 km) from the town of Ennis, 18 miles (29 km) from the city of Limerick. Ennis Train Station: 6 miles/10 km. Limerick Station: 18 miles/ 29 km. Shannon Int'l. Airport: 8 miles/13 km, 15 minutes.

Worldwide Reservations
www.preferredhotels.com
+800 323 7500   USA/Canada
+00 800 3237 5001   Europe (UIFN)
Other areas: See page 204

THE K CLUB

ACCOMMODATIONS: 79 total guestrooms, including 24 suites, each with two phones, voice mail, satellite TV, newspaper, robes, safe, fresh fruit, handmade chocolates, mineral water and VCR.

FACILITIES/SERVICES: Two 18-hole championship golf courses, spa, fitness center, river and course fishing, horseback riding, clay-target shooting, concierge, child care services, dry cleaning, salon, florist, shoe shine and shops. Golf and fishing classes available.

BUSINESS SERVICES: Secretarial service available.

DINING: "The Byerley Turk" offers fine dining blending French and Irish cuisine. The "Legends Restaurant" in the golf club offers à la carte choices in a relaxed atmosphere. Private dining available.

MEETINGS: Total Meeting Rooms: 4 Total Sq. Ft.: 4,844 / Sq. M.: 451

RATES: EUR 295.00 to 495.00; Corporate, Group, Package rates.

Mr. Ray Carroll, Chief Executive

Combining the elegance and unique charm of an Irish country house, The K Club is an elegantly restored 19th-century mansion estate nestled among 700 acres (283 hectares) of lush countryside. Guests will enjoy the luxurious surroundings of this warm, charming and intimate setting. On the River Liffey, 17 miles (27 km) southwest of Dublin. Venue for the Smurfit European Open and the Ryder Cup in 2006. Dublin Int'l. Airport: 15 miles/24 km, 30 minutes.

At Straffan
County Kildare , Ireland
Tel: +353 1601 7200
Fax: +353 1601 7299
Email: resortsales@kclub.ie
www.kclub.ie

Worldwide Reservations

www.preferredhotels.com

+800 323 7500 USA/Canada

+00 800 3237 5001 Europe (UIFN)

Other areas: See page 204

AGHADOE HEIGHTS HOTEL

ACCOMMODATIONS: 56 total guestrooms, including 8 suites, each with three telephones, Internet access, mini-bar, bathrobes, slippers, fresh fruit, handmade chocolates, flowers, mineral water, trouser press and satellite TV. Fax machine on request.

FACILITIES/SERVICES: Health club, swimming pool, sauna, plunge pool, solarium, Jacuzzi, fitness room, tennis, massage/treatment rooms, child care services, dry cleaning, concierge, limousine, jogging and walking trails, salon and valet parking.

BUSINESS SERVICES: On-site Business Center, complimentary Internet access, secretarial services and car rental services.

DINING: "Fredricks at the Heights" is renowned for its exquisite cuisine, including a full Irish breakfast and an extensive dinner menu. The "Heights" lounge offers a snack menu daily.

MEETINGS: Total Meeting Rooms: 3 Total Sq. Ft.: 2,861 / Sq. M.: 266

RATES: EUR 250.00 to 786.00; Corporate, Group, Package rates.

Mr. Pat Chawke, General Manager

Lakes of Killarney
Killarney, County Kerry, Ireland
Tel: +353 643 1766
Fax: +353 643 1345
Email: info@aghadoeheights.com
www.aghadoeheights.com

Situated in the South West of Ireland in the heart of County Kerry. Its glorious location on the hill of Aghadoe overlooking the Lakes of Killarney and the Kerry Mountains is unrivaled. The hotel is a haven of gracious elegance characterized by a treasure chest of antiques and contemporary design. The staff at Aghadoe pride themselves on their personal service to ensure that guests enjoy all the luxuries of an international 5-star hotel with a "country house" ambiance. Summer 2004, the hotel will open its new Spa and Wellness Center, 19 additional bedrooms and a spectacular Penthouse Suite. Kerry Airport: 9 miles/14 km, 15 minutes. Shannon Int'l. Airport 78 miles/125 km, 2 hours.

Worldwide Reservations
www.preferredhotels.com
+800 323 7500 USA/Canada
+00 800 3237 5001 Europe (UIFN)
Other areas: See page 204

145

PALAZZO ARZAGA HOTEL, SPA & GOLF RESORT

This unique property nestled on the hills overlooking Lake Garda enjoys a magnificent setting in acres of luscious landscape. A beautifully restored 15th-century country mansion, this hotel reflects the spirit of a past age with whitewashed walls, frescoed staircase, fireplaces, wooden beamed ceilings, antique furniture and richly adorned fabrics. Relax in a historic surrounding enriched by world-class golf and spa treatments. Situated in the province of Brescia. 20 minutes from Brescia-Montichiari Airport: 8 miles/20 km. 30 minutes from Verona-Catullo Airport: 27 miles/44 km. 90 minutes from Milan.

Worldwide Reservations

www.preferredhotels.com
+800 323 7500 USA/Canada
+00 800 3237 5001 Europe (UIFN)
Other areas: See page 204

ACCOMMODATIONS: 84 total guestrooms, including 3 suites, 1 junior suite, 2 fresco rooms. Some suites feature hand-painted ceilings, and all rooms feature mini-bar, safe, robes, data port, voice mail, hair dryer and satellite TV.

FACILITIES/SERVICES: Spa, thermal pool, treatment rooms, outdoor pool, tennis courts, golf with Jack Nicklaus II course and Gary Player course and pro shop. Arzaga Golf Academy, the teaching center of the PGA of Europe. Child care center is available.

BUSINESS SERVICES: Business facilities, airline ticketing and car rental.

DINING: Fine dining at "Il Moretto," featuring authentic atmosphere dishes. The "Clubhouse" cuisine offers informal buffet menus in a relaxed ambiance.

MEETINGS: Total Meeting Rooms: 5 Total Sq. Ft.: 3,918 / Sq. M.: 365

RATES: EUR 265.00 to 900.00; Corporate, Group, Package rates.

Mr. Giampaolo Burattin, Hotel Manager

25080 Carzago di Calvagese della Riviera
Desenzano 25080, Italy
Tel: +39 030 680 600
Fax: +39 030 680 6270
Email: arzaga@arzaga.it
www.palazzoarzaga.com

EXCELSIOR PALACE HOTEL

ACCOMMODATIONS: 131 total guestrooms, including 17 suites, each with two phones, high-speed Internet access, VCR on request, newspaper, safe, mini-bar, robes, hair dryer, slippers and satellite TV. CD player and fax machine available on request.

FACILITIES/SERVICES: Spa, concierge, shoe shine, fitness center, child care services, salon and dry cleaning.

BUSINESS SERVICES: Business Center and secretarial services.

DINING: "Lord Byron Restaurant" for the finest Italian food, "Eden Roc" in summer for local dishes with fresh fish. "Yachting Bar" for cocktails and "Sporting Bar" by the pool for low-calorie snacks and salads.

MEETINGS: Total Meeting Rooms: 9 Total Sq. Ft.: 6,997 / Sq. M.: 651

RATES: EUR 230.00 to 1,800.00; Corporate, Group, Package rates.

Mr. Aldo Werdin, General Manager

Via San Michele di Pagana, 8
Rapallo 16035, Italy
Tel: +39 0185 230666
Fax: +39 0185 230214
Email: excelsior@thi.it
www.excelsiorpalace.thi.it

Recently restored, this luxury hotel dates back to 1901 and perfectly combines its turn-of-the-century style with the comforts of a contemporary property. Uniquely located, overlooking the stunning Portofino Coast and the pretty bay of Rapallo, the hotel enjoys a breathtaking panoramic position. Experience the intimate beauty of this relaxing hideaway and its timeless elegance. Close to the well-known fishing village of Portofino and not far from the Cinque Terre area, part of UNESCO heritage. Genoa Airport: 20 miles/32 km, 45 minutes.

Worldwide Reservations
www.preferredhotels.com
+800 323 7500 USA/Canada
+00 800 3237 5001 Europe (UIFN)
Other areas: See page 204

PALAZZO SASSO

An elegant 12th-century villa situated on a clifftop 1,000 feet (305 meters) above the sparkling Mediterranean on the breathtaking Amalfi Coast. The historic hotel possesses a sense of timeless elegance — a civilized ambiance with a modern edge. On the Amalfi Coast close to the fishing village of Positano. Naples Airport: 37 miles/60 km, 90 minutes.

ACCOMMODATIONS: 44 total guestrooms, including 8 suites, all with Jacuzzi bath or shower, two phones, Internet connection, CD player, safe, hair dryer, mini-bar and robes. VCR and DVD on request.

FACILITIES/SERVICES: Rooftop sun terrace, swimming pool, tennis, gym area, hydromassage plunge pools, Internet station, concierge, garage, child care services, dry cleaning, shoe shine and massage. Planned private tours upon request.

BUSINESS SERVICES: Internet access available in the library. Secretarial and translating services available.

DINING: "Rossellinis" for Italian haute cuisine and "Caffé dell'Arte" for an array of local specialties. Awarded with one Michelin Star.

MEETINGS: Total Meeting Rooms: 1 Total Sq. Ft.: 1,033 / Sq. M.: 96

RATES: EUR 286.00 to 1,925.00;

Mr. Stefano Gegnacorsi, General Manager

Via San Giovanni del Toro, 28
Ravello 84010, Italy
Tel: +39 08 981 8181
Fax: +39 08 985 8900
Email: info@palazzosasso.com
www.palazzosasso.com

Worldwide Reservations
www.preferredhotels.com
+800 323 7500 USA/Canada
+00 800 3237 5001 Europe (UIFN)
Other areas: See page 204

SAN CLEMENTE PALACE

ACCOMMODATIONS: 205 total guestrooms, including 89 suites, each with two phones, data port, high-speed Internet access, VCR available on request, newspaper, safe, mini-bar, robes and hair dryer. Fax machine available in suites.

FACILITIES/SERVICES: Beauty & Wellness Club, tennis courts, a scenic outdoor pool, and a pitch and putt golf course to offer the hotel's clientele a chance to unwind with nature.

BUSINESS SERVICES: On-site Business Center, secretarial services and translating services available.

DINING: Four restaurants located on the most attractive points of the island offer tempting fare in the Mediterranean culinary tradition.

MEETINGS: Total Meeting Rooms: 6 Total Sq. Ft.: 3,423 / Sq. M.: 318

RATES: EUR 330.00 to 3,000.00; Corporate, Group, Package rates.

Mr. Maurizio D'Este,
General Manager

Isola di San Clemente, 1, San Marco
Venice 30124, Italy
Tel: +39 041 2445001
Fax: +39 041 2445800
Email: sanclemente@thi.it
www.sanclemente.thi.it

The restoration has made it possible to preserve the historical flavor of the Renaissance and to achieve a luxurious hotel for guests who expect the best. Venice's new luxury hotel, exclusively located on the island of San Clemente, is an oasis of peace, with an enchanting view of the lagoon. Centrally located only a few minutes away from St. Mark's Square by the 24-hour complimentary shuttle boat, 15 minutes away from both the car park and railway station. Marco Polo Int'l Airport: 10 miles/16 km, 30 minutes.

Worldwide Reservations
www.preferredhotels.com
+800 323 7500 USA/Canada
+00 800 3237 5001 Europe (UIFN)
Other areas: See page 204

HOTEL PORT PALACE

Located in the heart of
Monte Carlo at the base of
the Casino, the contemporary
and elegant Port Palace
provides guests both comfort
and style in this magnificent
Mediterranean locale overlooking the picturesque harbor
of Monaco. In the heart
of Monte Carlo, the resort is
a 45-minute drive and a
7-minute helicopter flight from
Nice Int'l. Airport. The Monte
Carlo train station is only a
few steps away from the hotel.

ACCOMMODATIONS: 50 suites,
each with two multi-line phones,
high-speed Internet access, voice
mail, VCR on request, newspaper,
safe, mini-bar, robes, hair dryer, fax
on request, plasma TV, and Jacuzzi.
Four suites feature Turkish baths.

FACILITIES/SERVICES: Guest
services, fitness center, beauty salon,
dry cleaning. Child care services,
parking, and transfer service available
on request.

BUSINESS SERVICES: Secretarial
and translating services, audiovisual
material rental, faxing and copying
all available on request.

DINING: The Port Palace features
two bars along with the gastronomic
restaurant the "Grand Large" and
"La Réserve", a wine club.

MEETINGS: Total Meeting Rooms: 3
Total Sq. Ft.: 1,421 / Sq. M.: 132

RATES: EUR 600.00 to 2,100.00;
Corporate, Group, Package rates.

Mr. Eric Pere, General Manager

7 Ave. John F. Kennedy
Monte Carlo 98000, Monaco
Tel: +377 9 797 9000
Fax: +377 9 797 9001
Email: reservation@portpalace.com
www.portpalace.com

Worldwide Reservations
www.preferredhotels.com
+800 323 7500 USA/Canada
+00 800 3237 5001 Europe (UIFN)
Other areas: See page 204

GRAND HOTEL HUIS TER DUIN

ACCOMMODATIONS: 254 total guestrooms, including 22 suites, and 4 penthouses, each offering modern conveniences, with views of the North Sea or the charming bulb area of Noordwijk.

FACILITIES/SERVICES: Laundry service, indoor pool, sauna, Turkish health bath, fitness center, massage, solarium, spa, salon, business floor, high-speed Internet facilities, billiard room, mini-golf, tennis, beach pavilion, concierge, shuttle service and heliport.

BUSINESS SERVICES: Business Center.

DINING: Grand Hotel Huis ter Duin has two fine dining restaurants. The prestigious "Restaurant Latour" serves French cuisine; "La Terrasse" serves casual lunches or dinners.

MEETINGS: Total Meeting Rooms: 19 Total Sq. Ft.: 41,505 / Sq. M.: 3,864

RATES: EUR 260.00 to 1425.00; Corporate, Group, Package rates.

Mr. Stephan J. A. B. Stokkermans, Commercial Director

Koningin Astrid Blvd. 5, P.O. Box 85, 2200 AB
Noordwijk aan Zee , The Netherlands
Tel: +31 71 361 9220
Fax: +31 71 361 9401
Email: info@huisterduin.com
www.huisterduin.com

The fashionable family owned and managed Grand Hotel Huis ter Duin has a long-established international reputation. Superbly situated on top of the dunes directly on the beach, this majestic hotel offers a marvelous view of the North Sea. The shine of polished marble and natural stone reflects the grandeur of the entrance, lobby and public rooms. Centrally located between Amsterdam, The Hague and Leiden. Amsterdam Schiphol Airport is only: 20 miles/32 km, 20 minutes.

BEAU-RIVAGE, GENEVA

Built in 1865, the very private Beau-Rivage still plays host to those who shape our world. Charm and discretion combine with efficient service, modern comfort and amenities, making this unique hotel one of the most distinguished addresses in Switzerland. It boasts views of the lake and the Alps and it is just a stroll away from the shopping and business district. In the heart of the city center, it faces the lake and Mont Blanc and is close to the United Nations. International Airport (Geneva Cointrin): 3 miles/5 km, 15 minutes.

ACCOMMODATIONS: 93 total guestrooms, including 11 suites, renovated and decorated by designer Leila Corbett. Bathrobes, trouser press, mini-bar. New Genesis interactive TV system by Quadriga with Video on Demand (DVD options), CD jukebox and Internet access with wireless keyboards.

FACILITIES/SERVICES: Child care services, concierge, dry cleaning, shoe shine, limousine and concierge.

BUSINESS SERVICES: Each room with two multi-line phones, data port, voice mail, fax, newspaper, high-speed Internet connection with VPN (512 Kbps). Wireless connections in all meeting rooms and public areas. Business Center and secretarial services. Video-conferences on request.

DINING: "Le Chat-Botte," a world-renowned French restaurant; "Atrium Bar" with afternoon tea, cocktails and piano entertainment; "Patara," fine Thai cuisine.

MEETINGS: Total Meeting Rooms: 6 Total Sq. Ft.: 5,844 / Sq. M.: 543

RATES: CHF 480.00 to 3,300.00; Corporate, Group, Package rates.

Mr. Jacques Mayer, Managing Director

13, quai du Mont-Blanc
Geneva CH-1201, Switzerland
Tel: +41 22 716 6666
Fax: +41 22 716 6060
Email: info@beau-rivage.ch
www.beau-rivage.ch

Worldwide Reservations
www.preferredhotels.com
+800 323 7500 USA/Canada
+00 800 3237 5001 Europe (UIFN)
Other areas: See page 204

PARK HOTEL VITZNAU

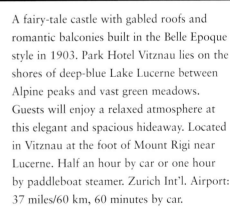

ACCOMMODATIONS: 103 total guestrooms, including 32 suites, some with mini-bar, safe, robes, hair dryer, data port, voice mail and ISDN connections. Fax and VCR upon request.

FACILITIES/SERVICES: Beauty and Wellness Center, heated indoor/ outdoor pool, sauna, steam bath, massage, energy therapy, fitness center, hiking, biking, concierge, child care services, dry cleaning, shoe shine and nearby salon. Golf, fishing, scuba diving, snorkeling, wind-surfing and horseback riding nearby.

BUSINESS SERVICES: On-site Business Center, secretarial services and translating services available.

DINING: The "Panoramarestaurant," with a breathtaking view of Lake Lucerne, offers international cuisine. "Quatre Cantons" offers contemporary cuisine. Both have musical entertainment. The pool terrace offers lunch, snacks and charcoal-grilled dishes.

MEETINGS: Total Meeting Rooms: 9 Total Sq. Ft.: 1,560 / Sq. M.: 145

RATES: CHF 360.00 to 1,750.00; Group rates.

Mr. Peter Bally, Managing Director

@

Vitznau CH-6354, Switzerland
Tel: +41 41 399 60 60
Fax: +41 41 399 60 70
Email: info@phv.ch
www.parkhotel-vitznau.ch

A fairy-tale castle with gabled roofs and romantic balconies built in the Belle Epoque style in 1903. Park Hotel Vitznau lies on the shores of deep-blue Lake Lucerne between Alpine peaks and vast green meadows. Guests will enjoy a relaxed atmosphere at this elegant and spacious hideaway. Located in Vitznau at the foot of Mount Rigi near Lucerne. Half an hour by car or one hour by paddleboat steamer. Zurich Int'l. Airport: 37 miles/60 km, 60 minutes by car.

Worldwide Reservations
www.preferredhotels.com
+800 323 7500 USA/Canada
+00 800 3237 5001 Europe (UIFN)
Other areas: See page 204

SWISS DIAMOND HOTEL OLIVELLA

This recently restored Italian-style hotel, is situated on the shores of Lake Lugano just 7 km from downtown Lugano. Elegant and warm, it is a relaxing oasis for a relaxing getaway. Venus Wellness Center, Fitness Center. For your well-being, Health Institute Henri Chenot is a new concept of health, a concept strictly linked to the progressive evolution of aging. Water sports, exclusive yacht for private meetings or excursions. Milan Int'l. Airport: 34 miles/ 55 km, 30 minutes.

ACCOMMODATIONS: 88 total guestrooms, including 7 suites, each with wireless high-speed Internet access, satellite TV, two phones, voice mail, safe, mini-bar, robes and hair dryer. VCR available upon request.

FACILITIES/SERVICES: Spa, concierge, shoe shine, fitness center, child care services, salon, dry cleaning, florist and shops. Water sports, boat rentals. Lake garden, outdoor pool and Jacuzzi.

DINING: "Panorama" features gastronomic fare; "des Artistes" features Italian specialties; "al lago" specializes in Mediterranean cuisine.

MEETINGS: Total Meeting Rooms: 5 Total Sq. Ft.: 2,799 / Sq. M.: 260

RATES: CHF 220.00 to 1,600.00; Corporate, Group, Package rates.

Mr. Francesco Cirillo, General Manager

6921 Vico Morcote
Lugano, Switzerland
Tel: +41 91 735 00 00
Fax: +41 91 735 00 99
Email: info@swissdiamondhotel.com
www.swissdiamondhotel.com

Worldwide Reservations
www.preferredhotels.com
+800 323 7500   USA/Canada
+00 800 3237 5001   Europe (UIFN)
Other areas: See page 204

THE CARLTON HOTEL

ACCOMMODATIONS: 105 total guestrooms, including 6 suites, each with complimentary newspaper, safe, mini-bar, TV, radio and hair dryer.

FACILITIES/SERVICES: Spa, health club, concierge, child care services, shoe shine, dry cleaning and salon.

BUSINESS SERVICES: Secretarial services available.

DINING: "Restaurant Le Romanoff" is an elegant dining room where the stunning view provides a perfect accompaniment to culinary delights; "Restaurant Tschine," a cozy à la carte restaurant, features regional and international cuisine. The hotel also features a bar with fireplace and piano.

MEETINGS: Total Meeting Rooms: 4 Total Sq. Ft.: 4,844 / Sq. M.: 451

RATES: CHF 160.00 to 1,070.00; Group, Package rates.

Mr. Dominic Bachofen,
General Manager

Via J. Badrutt 11
7500 St. Moritz, Switzerland
Tel: +41 81 836 70 00
Fax: +41 81 836 70 01
Email: info@carlton-stmoritz.ch
www.carlton-stmoritz.ch

This elegant building was built in 1913 in a remarkably beautiful setting, and it has been completely renovated to blend tradition, personalized service and modern sophistication. Located in the sunniest area of St. Moritz, it is a few minutes' walk from the village center. The rooms offer spectacular views of the St. Moritz lake and mountains. Within five minutes' walking distance to the city center, shopping, restaurants, bars, cinema and casino. Zurich Int'l. Airport: 125 miles/200 km, 3 hours. Samedan Airport: 4 miles/6 km, 10 minutes.

Worldwide Reservations
www.preferredhotels.com
+800 323 7500 USA/Canada
+00 800 3237 5001 Europe (UIFN)
Other areas: See page 204

GRAND HOTEL ZERMATTERHOF

Set in a private park with a view of the Matterhorn, this historic hotel has recently been renovated to satisfy every guest expectation. Designed to complement its Alpine furnishings, two-thirds of the rooms offer majestic mountain views. In the center of Zermatt, close to skiing, shopping and nightlife. Milan Int'l. Airport: 137 miles/ 220 km, 180 minutes. Geneva Airport: 155 miles/250 km, 180 minutes.

ACCOMMODATIONS: 84 total guestrooms, including 26 suites, each with phones, voice mail, data port, VOD, Sony PlayStation, Internet access via TV, safe, robes and mini-bar. VCR on request.

FACILITIES/SERVICES: Indoor pool, Jacuzzi, sauna, steam room, massage, fitness center, concierge and child care services.

BUSINESS SERVICES: Limited business services available.

DINING: Choose from two restaurants and two bars, including formal dining in "Prato Borni," informal dining in the new terrace restaurant, "Lusi," culinary delights with a Mediterranean touch.

MEETINGS: Total Meeting Rooms: 5 Total Sq. Ft.: 5,400 / Sq. M.: 503

RATES: CHF 290.00 to 1,870.00; Corporate, Group, Package rates.

Mr. Jean-Pierre Lanz,
General Manager

Bahnhofstrasse 55, Postfach 14
Zermatt CH-3920, Switzerland
Tel: +41 27 966 6600
Fax: +41 27 966 6699
Email: info@zermatterhof.ch
www.zermatterhof.ch

THE LANDMARK LONDON

ACCOMMODATIONS: 299 total guestrooms, including 47 suites, each with three multi-line phones, data port, voice mail, VCR/DVD on request, newspaper, safe, mini-bar, robes, hair dryer and marble bathrooms.

FACILITIES/SERVICES: E'SPA treatments and massages, 50-foot (15-meter) pool, spa, saunas, steam room and salon.

BUSINESS SERVICES: 24-hour Business Center, secretarial and translating services available.

DINING: The spectacular "Winter Garden" is famous for its award-winning afternoon tea and exquisite setting. Enjoy a relaxed meal in the traditional "Cellars Bar and Restaurant," which offers an extensive range of international beer, wines and cigars.

MEETINGS: Total Meeting Rooms: 11 Total Sq. Ft.: 16,815 / Sq. M.: 1,565

RATES: GBP 330.00 to 1,565.00; Corporate, Group, Package rates.

Mr. Francis Green, General Manager

222 Marylebone Road
London NW1 6JQ, United Kingdom
Tel: +44 207 631 8000
Fax: +44 207 631 8080
Email: reservations@thelandmark.co.uk
www.landmarklondon.co.uk

The Landmark London, winner of the Best Hotel in London 2003 award, offers the largest guestrooms in London, each an oasis of peace and serenity in the heart of the capital. Located in fashionable Marylebone, the new Notting Hill, The Landmark London sits with the famous West End on its doorstep. Heathrow Int'l. Airport: 15 miles/24 km, 15 minutes, via Heathrow Express train.

Worldwide Reservations
www.preferredhotels.com
+800 323 7500 USA/Canada
+00 800 3237 5001 Europe (UIFN)
Other areas: See page 204

At Your Service

Sleep in, relax, order room service — at Preferred hotels and resorts, we live to serve. We don't just cater to your every whim, we dream up new ones.

PREFERRED
HOTELS & RESORTS
WORLD WIDE

THE LANESBOROUGH

ACCOMMODATIONS: 95 total guestrooms, including 46 suites, each with complimentary Internet and email access along with free access to extensive film and CD libraries. Complimentary butler service, DVD players, three phones (one cordless and two with multiple lines), data port, voice mail, VCR on request, newspaper, fax machine, butler trays, safe, robes, hair dryer.

FACILITIES/SERVICES: Newly opened spa and fitness center, concierge, shoe shine, child care services, dry cleaning and florist.

BUSINESS SERVICES: On-site Business Center, secretarial and translating services.

DINING: "The Conservatory" offers innovative cuisine, featuring Pacific Rim and Mediterranean flavors. The "Library" and "Withdrawing Room" are available for drinks in a traditional English club setting.

MEETINGS: Total Meeting Rooms: 6 Total Sq. Ft.: 5,210 / Sq. M.: 485

RATES: GBP 285.00 to 5,000.00; Group, Package rates.

Mr. Geoffrey A. Gelardi, Managing Director

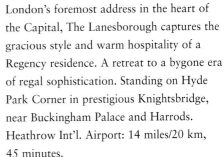

London's foremost address in the heart of the Capital, The Lanesborough captures the gracious style and warm hospitality of a Regency residence. A retreat to a bygone era of regal sophistication. Standing on Hyde Park Corner in prestigious Knightsbridge, near Buckingham Palace and Harrods. Heathrow Int'l. Airport: 14 miles/20 km, 45 minutes.

Hyde Park Corner
London SW1X 7TA, United Kingdom
Tel: +44 20 7259 5599
Fax: +44 20 7259 5606
Email: info@lanesborough.com
www.lanesborough.com

Worldwide Reservations
www.preferredhotels.com
+800 323 7500   USA/Canada
+00 800 3237 5001   Europe (UIFN)
Other areas: See page 204

159

ST ANDREWS BAY GOLF RESORT & SPA

St Andrews, Scotland, United Kingdom

ACCOMMODATIONS: 209 total guestrooms, including 17 suites, each with voice mail, data port, high-speed Internet access, CD/DVD players, newspaper, robes, hair dryer, mini-bar and in-house movies.

FACILITIES/SERVICES: Two magnificent golf courses, The Torrance and The Devlin, weave their way over the rolling landscape providing an unforgettable experience for any golfer. For pampering off the tees, the spa indulges the body and soul.

BUSINESS SERVICES: Business Center and secretarial services available.

DINING: Formal dining in the relaxed environment of "The Squire." "Kittock's Den" provides a cozy setting. "The Clubhouse" has panoramic views for a stunning dining experience with traditional club fare. Opening in 2005, "Esperante" is a Tuscan-influenced fine dining restaurant.

MEETINGS: Total Meeting Rooms: 15 Total Sq. Ft.: 15,000 / Sq. M.: 1,396

RATES: GBP 180.00 to 270.00; Corporate, Group, Package rates.

Mr. Stephen Carter, General Manager

St Andrews Bay Golf Resort & Spa sits proudly amidst the rugged, coastal landscape of the silvery River Tay with spectacular views of the bay's golden beaches and medieval skyline. St Andrews Bay offers an international standard of service and meticulous attention to detail in the comfort and convenience of a modern world-class resort shrouded in the history of the "Home of Golf." Situated just 1.5 miles/ 2.4 km from downtown St Andrews. Leuchars train station: 7 miles/11 km. Edinburgh Int'l. Airport: 50 miles/80 km, 50 minutes.

St Andrews
Fife KY16 8PN, United Kingdom
Tel: +44 1 334 837000
Fax: +44 1 334 471115
Email: info@standrewsbay.com
www.standrewsbay.com

Worldwide Reservations
www.preferredhotels.com
***+800 323 7500** USA/Canada*
***+00 800 3237 5001** Europe (UIFN)*
Other areas: See page 204

Africa

PALMERAIE GOLF PALACE & RESORT

This unique palace, built in the traditional Marrakchi style, is a door opened on the Moroccan culture and architecture. Relax in this luxurious resort nestled in a legendary palm grove. Experience a warm and friendly atmosphere in a peaceful and elegant place. 10 minutes away from the city center, in the protected palm grove of Marrakech. This deluxe hotel is surrounded by a beautiful 18-hole golf course designed by Robert Trent Jones, Sr. Menara Marrakech Airport: 9 miles/15 km, 15 minutes.

ACCOMMODATIONS: 314 total guestrooms, including 28 suites, each with two phones, newspaper, safe, mini-bar, robes, hair dryer and bottled water.

FACILITIES/SERVICES: Sauna, hammam, Jacuzzi, spa, concierge, shoe shine, fitness center, child care services, salon, tennis, dry cleaning, shops, horseback riding, squash and 18-hole golf course.

BUSINESS SERVICES: On-site Business Center, secretarial services, and translating services on request. Registered address and office rental available.

DINING: The hotel offers 10 restaurants, four bars and a discotheque for your dining pleasure.

MEETINGS: Total Meeting Rooms: 16 Total Sq. Ft.: 17,426 / Sq. M.: 1,622

RATES: MAD 3,100.00 to 4,000.00; Corporate, Group, Package rates.

Mr. Jacques Bouriot,
General Manager

Les Jardins de la Palmeraie, Circuit de la Palmeraie, P.O. Box 1488 Marrakech , Morocco
Tel: +212 44 30 10 10
Fax: +212 44 30 20 20
Email: reservation@pgp.ma
www.pgpmarrakech.com

Worldwide Reservations
www.preferredhotels.com
+800 323 7500 USA/Canada
+00 800 3237 5001 Europe (UIFN)
Other areas: See page 204

FANCOURT HOTEL & COUNTRY CLUB ESTATE

ACCOMMODATIONS: 150 total guestrooms, including 85 suites, each with two phones, voice mail, mini-bar, newspaper, safe, robes, tea/coffee, Internet connection and hair dryer. VCR on request.

FACILITIES/SERVICES: Four Gary Player courses, including the exciting new Links course (host to the President's Cup 2003), Golf Academy, tennis courts, snooker room, fitness center, spa, child care services, dry cleaning, shoe shine, salon, swimming pools, lawn bowling, cinema and walking trail.

BUSINESS SERVICES: Business Center, secretarial and translating services.

DINING: Italian in "La Cantina," healthy cuisine in the "Morning Glory," seafood in "Le Pêcheur," African dishes at "Sansibar" and fusion cuisine in "Bramble Lodge."

MEETINGS: Total Meeting Rooms: 7 Total Sq. Ft.: 11,840 / Sq. M.: 1,102

RATES: ZAR 1,540.00 to 6,175.00; Corporate, Group, Package rates.

Mr. Steven Thielke,
Hotel General Manager

  @

Montagu Street, Blanco, P.O. Box 2266
George 6530, South Africa
Tel: +27 44 804 0000
Fax: +27 44 804 0700
Email: hotel@fancourt.co.za
www.fancourt.com

Fancourt offers a combination of old-world charm and contemporary luxury on 1,137 acres (515 hectares) of lush countryside with the Outeniqua Mountains as its backdrop. Guests will cherish each moment in this haven of tranquility and style. Situated in the heart of the Garden Route. George Airport: 4.3 miles/7 km, 7 minutes. Cape Town Airport: 260 miles/420 km, 4 hours.

Worldwide Reservations
www.preferredhotels.com
+800 323 7500 USA/Canada
+00 800 3237 5001 Europe (UIFN)
Other areas: See page 204

Asia·Pacific